Lakeland Rocks and Landscape
A Field Guide

The Cumberland Geological Society is a highly regarded scientific society interested in all aspects of geology in the County of Cumbria and surrounding areas.

Members receive regular newsletters, and every two years the Society publishes its Proceedings. These contain original papers, together with summaries of excursions and lectures. From April to September, a full programme of geological excursions is arranged, while from September through to March, there are monthly lectures.

Membership is open to anyone with an interest in geology and newcomers are welcome. The publishers will be pleased to advise the address of the current Secretary.

LAKELAND ROCKS AND LANDSCAPE

A FIELD GUIDE

THE CUMBERLAND GEOLOGICAL SOCIETY

•

Edited by Mervyn Dodd

Ellenbank
Press

Published by Ellenbank Press
Park Hill South
Camp Road
Maryport
Cumbria CA15 6JN

First published as *The Lake District* by Unwin
Paperbacks in 1982
This substantially revised and enlarged edition
published by Ellenbank Press 1992

Reprinted 1992, 1995, 1996, 1998

Designed by Sheila Sherwen

Typeset in Linotron Baskerville by
Deltatype Ltd, Ellesmere Port, Cheshire
Printed and bound in Great Britain by
Anthenaeum Press Ltd, Gateshead, Tyne & Wear.

British Library Cataloguing in Publication Data
A catalogue record for this book is available
from the British Library.

ISBN 1–873551–03–7

Contents

Foreword *Chris Bonington*   vii

Preface and Acknowledgements   viii-ix

Geological Background *Alan Smith*   1

Field Excursions

1   Lower Carboniferous rocks near Orton, east of Shap
Alan Day   12

2   The Shap Granite *Eric Skipsey*   19

3   Windermere Group rocks around Tarn Hows
John Gunner   26

4   The Carboniferous Limestones of Low Furness
David Kelly   34

5   The Windermere Group south of Torver *David Kelly*   41

6   The Eskdale Granite *Brian Young*   46

7   Volcanic rocks of northern Wasdale *Mike Petterson*   54

8   The Permo-Trias of St Bees Headland *Tom Shipp*   62

9   The Lower Palaeozoic rocks of the Buttermere Valley
Mervyn Dodd   69

10   Glacial features at Rosthwaite in Borrowdale
Ken Bond   75

11   The Armboth Dyke, Thirlmere *Morley Burton*   83

Contents

12 Quaternary features north of the Kirkstone Pass
    Richard Clark   88

13 Landscape development near Keswick
    John Boardman   95

14 The Skiddaw Granite north of Threlkeld *Tom Shipp*   101

15 The Carboniferous Limestone between Caldbeck
    and Uldale *Tom Shipp*   107

16 The Penrith Sandstone of the Vale of Eden
    Jim Cockersole   115

17 Palaeozoic rocks of the Cross Fell district
    Eric Skipsey   123

18 The Lower Carboniferous rocks of West Edenside
    Alan Day   130

Glossary   134

Geological and Mineralogical Museum Collections
in Cumbria   143

Further Reading   146

Index   148

Foreword

I am no geologist but rocks have played an overwhelming part in my life from the age of sixteen when I first set foot on the crags of Snowdonia. Since then I have been lucky enough to climb on rocks of every sort, from the active volcano, Sangay, in Ecuador, to the remote Mount Vinson in Antarctica and the great peaks of the Himalaya, with many, many others in between.

Nevertheless there is nowhere other than the English Lake District where I would choose to live. Not only is the scenery outstandingly beautiful but I am fascinated by the way that man has left his mark on the landscape, and one of the major reasons for this is its diversity of rocks and minerals. Man has used these from ancient times and left evidence of his use, in implements such as axe heads, religious monuments like Castlerigg Stone Circle, in the remains of the earliest hut circles, in the patchwork of stone walls used for farming and, of course, in numerous mines and quarries.

I live on the edge of the Caldbeck Fells which were extensively mined, in some parts until very recently, and when the wind is lashing the sleet against my window I often think what it must have been like for the early miners and quarrymen in such conditions.

To know how the landscape has been formed geologically adds another dimension to our appreciation of the fells, and this very readable book offers an insight for a layman like myself. It contains some fascinating excursions covering the Lake District in its widest sense, going as far east as Shap and the Eden Valley, and right across to St Bees Head in the west (where I pioneered some new rock-climbing routes twenty-six years ago).

But in furthering our knowledge and appreciation, we must remember that we are the guardians of this unique area. We need to protect the Lake District from pollution and damage so that it can be handed on to future generations with its rare beauty intact. If possible, we should try to leave it in even better condition than that in which we have been privileged to know it.

Chris Bonington, March 1991

Preface

Like *The Lake District*, published in 1982, this book has been written by members and friends of the Cumberland Geological Society. The contributors, amateurs and professionals alike, are united by their knowledge and enthusiasm for the areas they describe and explain. So many challenging new ideas about the origin of Lake District rocks and landscapes have been developed recently that a new book is essential. In particular the work of the British Geological Survey over the last decade has provided exciting new perspectives, especially in providing a better understanding of the volcanic rocks and more coherent accounts of the events that produced the sedimentary rocks of the Windermere and Skiddaw Groups.

We begin with 'The Geological Background', a very readable account of the events which produced the features we describe in the excursion chapters. There are 18 of these, ranging from Caldbeck to Shap, and from the Vale of Eden to St Bees Head. Half of these are new chapters, focussing mainly on the landscapes of the Central and Southern Lakes. The others are revised and rewritten excursions to some of the areas the 1982 book described. Each excursion chapter is self-contained, and all have been walked independently to check the accuracy of our route-finding instructions. Details of parking facilities and where to seek permission for access are given. The Glossary provides brief explanations of the terms that appear in bold type in the text. Finally, Further Reading selects the more readable and accessible books and periodicals about the Lake District; some for the beginner and some for the more knowledgeable.

This book is for the interested amateur with some background knowledge of the earth sciences, and for field study groups. The Lake District is very much the jewel in the crown of English upland landscapes. Do help to conserve it for future visitors and residents! Please remember the obvious – like closing gates, not dropping litter, driving carefully and thoughtfully, and collecting specimens from broken fragments instead of hammering rock faces. Above all, use this book and enjoy exploring the geology of the Lake District.

Mervyn Dodd, Cumberland Geological Society

Acknowledgements

I greatly appreciate the advice and encouragement received from Ken Bond, Iver Gray, Tom Shipp and Eric Skipsey, fellow members of the Cumberland Geological Society, during the editing of this book. Officers of the British Geological Survey, Newcastle upon Tyne, have given very helpful guidance and Dr Ben Kneller of the Department of Earth Sciences, the University of Liverpool, has generously allowed us to use his papers, published and unpublished, on the stratigraphy of the Windermere Group. Finally I would like to thank the many members and friends of the Cumberland Geological Society who have so willingly walked the excursion routes in this book.

Note: The details of routes given in this guide do not imply a right of way. Readers are reminded to seek permission where necessary both to use footpaths and to gain access to exposures.

Every effort has been made to ensure that the information presented in this book is accurate and up to date. However, if you find any changes that you feel should be included in the next edition, the publishers will be pleased to hear from you.

Notes on safety have been included in this guide but readers are reminded that the publishers and the Society cannot take responsibility for accident or injury sustained on the excursion routes. Care should always be taken to check weather conditions before setting out on the excursions, especially in remote or hilly areas.

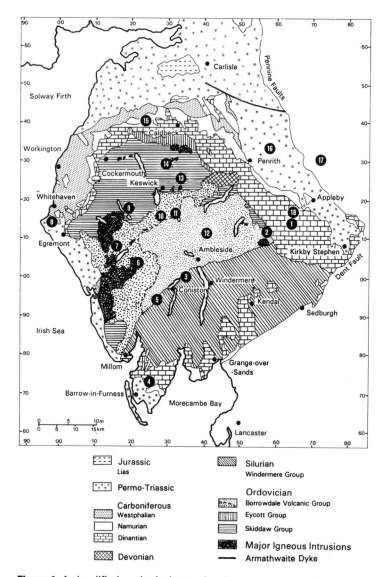

Figure 1 A simplified geological map showing the excursion locations.

Geological Background

Alan Smith *General Secretary, Cumberland Geological Society and formerly Director, North Cheshire College of Higher and Further Education*

It has taken over 500 million years of earth history to create the Lake District, the first 100 million years overshadowing everything that followed. This was when the major rock groups formed and were then uplifted into the mighty **Caledonian** mountain range whose eroded remnants form the present-day Lake District.

The Lake District is a small dome of Lower Palaeozoic (Ordovician and Silurian) rocks, an **inlier** protruding from beneath a cover of Carboniferous and Permo-Triassic rocks. The edge of the Lower Palaeozoic core is almost everywhere marked by a distinct change of slope. The Lake District National Park boundaries and the 250 m contour (where the hills begin) coincide with this noticeable change in geology.

Figure 1 is a geological sketch map of the district and locates the excursions described in this guide. Table 1 is the detailed geological succession which will help in following this introduction and the excursion chapters. Table 2 takes a more general approach to the geological history. Terms printed in **bold** are explained in the Glossary (p. 135).

THE LOWER PALAEOZOIC CORE
The Skiddaw Group

Skiddaw Group rocks are the oldest in the district, forming almost a third of the mountain core, and outcropping in a wide belt in the northern and western fells. They also form Black Combe in the extreme southwest and appear as inliers around the lower reaches of Ullswater and Haweswater. Further east they reappear at the foot of the Pennine Escarpment below Cross Fell.

These rocks are very difficult to interpret. They are mainly

Stratigraphical divisions		Principal lithological groups and formations		
QUATERNARY Devensian		glacial deposits		
JURASSIC Liassic		calcareous shales		
TRIASSIC		MERCIA MUDSTONE GROUP	Stanwix Shales	
		SHERWOOD SANDSTONE GROUP	Kirklinton Sandstone St Bees Sandstone	
PERMIAN	upper		Eden Shale, St Bees Shale with evaporites	
	lower		Penrith Sandstone, Brockram	
CARBONIFEROUS	Westphalian	COAL MEASURES	upper (barren, red beds) middle lower	
	Namurian	MILLSTONE GRIT	Roosecote Mudstone Hensingham Grit First Limestone	
	Dinantian	CARBONIFEROUS LIMESTONE	Gleaston Formation Urswick Limestone Park Limestone Dalton Beds Red Hill Oölite Basement Beds	2nd Limestone 3rd Limestone 4th Limestone 5th Limestone 6th Limestone Cockermouth Lavas Basement Beds
DEVONIAN		Mell Fell Conglomerate		
SILURIAN	Pridoli Ludlow		Scout Hill Formation	
			Kirkby Moor Formation Underbarrow Formation Bannisdale Formation Coniston Subgroup	
	Wenlock Llandovery	WINDERMERE	Tranearth Subgroup Stockdale Subgroup	
ORDOVICIAN	Ashgill	GROUP	Dent Subgroup	
	Caradoc––Llandeilo	BORROWDALE VOLCANIC GROUP	UPPER Yewdale Breccia Tilberthwaite Tuff Seathwaite Fells Tuff Airy's Bridge Formation LOWER Birker Fell Andesites Honister Tuff	
	Llanvirn	EYCOTT GROUP		
	Arenig	SKIDDAW GROUP	Kirk Stile Slates Loweswater Flags Hope Beck Slates	

Igneous intrusive rocks, mainly associated with the Caledonian orogeny

granites	Skiddaw, Shap, Eskdale	diorite	
granophyres	Buttermere and Ennerdale, Carrock Fell	microgranite dolerite	occurring as sills, dykes and volcanic necks
microgranite	Threlkeld	picrite	
gabbro	Carrock Fell	minette	

Table 1 The geological succession in the Lake District and surrounding areas.

Stratigraphic Groups	Principal Local Formations	Major Events
Lower Palaeozoic (600–405 Ma)		
ORDOVICIAN 510–450 Ma	The Skiddaw Group (510–460 Ma) of the northern and western Lake District.	Deep-sea mudstones and sandstones laid down as the Iapetus Ocean narrowed.
	The Borrowdale Volcanic Group (460–450 Ma) of the central Lake District.	Increasingly violent eruptions on land and in shallow water as the ocean crust was subducted.
SILURIAN 450–405 Ma	The Windermere Group of the southern Lake District.	Shales and sandstones deposited in seas deepening as the Iapetus Ocean closed.
Upper Palaeozoic (405–250 Ma)		
DEVONIAN 405–355 Ma	Caledonian mountain building and granite intrusions.	Continental collision produced mountain ranges followed by rapid erosion.
CARBONIFEROUS 355–290 Ma	Carboniferous Limestones around and possibly over the Lake District (355–320 Ma).	Shallow, clear seas in tropical latitudes with coral reefs.
	Coal Measures in West Cumbria.	Tropical rain forests and extensive deltas.
290 +/− 10 Ma	Hercynian mountain building.	Continental collision and uplift of Lake District.
PERMO-TRIASSIC 290–205 Ma	The New Red Rocks of West Cumbria, the Vale of Eden, near Carlisle and around Barrow.	Hot desert climates. Deposition on land, in shallow salt lakes and seas.
MESOZOIC and TERTIARY 205–2 Ma	No rocks of these ages remain in the Lake District.	The Lake District was land.
PLEISTOCENE last 2 million years	Glacial and Inter-glacial deposits.	Rapid climatic change. Glacial, tundra and interglacial climate.

Table 2 An outline geological history showing principal formations and events. Ma = millions of years before present.

greywackes, siltstones, mudstones (some now **slates**) with sand-stones. They were deposited by **turbidity currents** on the continental slopes of the former **Iapetus** ocean. They are more than 3000 m thick and were laid down in relatively deep water over a long period of time. Their monotonous and uniform grey colour makes them difficult to interpret.

Structurally they are very complex. Besides having undergone many phases of folding, they are also highly **cleaved** (hence the old name, Skiddaw Slates) and altered by **thermal metamorphism** and mineralization. How far their structures are due to their original setting and how far a result of later upheaval in the Caledonian **orogeny** is debatable. Small-scale slumping undoubtedly occurred on the continental slope. Large rafts of rock (olistoliths) up to 0.5 km long have been found near Buttermere. These appear to have slid down the continental slope, creating chaotic jumbles of material where they finally halted.

Fossils are rare in the Skiddaw Group. For over a century the rock sequences were identified by their graptolite assemblages. Recently the discovery of **achritarchs** and other micro-fossils has provided a new approach.

There are distinct zones in the Skiddaw Group separated by major east-northeast trending faults. One major fault zone crosses the northwestern fells from the Crummock Water area through Causey Pike. North of this **thrust fault**, slump structures due to movements on the continental slopes dominate; whereas to the south, complex mixtures of rock with many olistoliths are usual.

Excursion 9 to the Buttermere valley introduces these rocks. It illustrates their lithology and structures, visiting locations on both sides of the Causey Pike Thrust Fault.

Ordovician Volcanic Rocks

Volcanic rocks succeed the Skiddaw Group, indicating new environmental conditions. These changes were taking place because the Iapetus Ocean was narrowing as the American and European tectonic plates drifted towards one another during the Ordovician Period. Eventually the American plate subducted (buckled under) and ocean floor sediments of the Skiddaw Group were forced upwards. Island arc volcanic activity took place along this active plate margin, as in present-day Japan. The processes which built the Caledonian mountain chains had begun.

The volcanics are exciting, highly variable rocks, reflecting the most dramatic episode of Lake District geological history. They are not easy to map and interpret, partly because volcanoes, by their very nature, behave fitfully and erratically. Distinct phases can be recognized. The oldest is the Eycott Group which may have been erupted partly in submarine conditions as some of the last Skiddaw Group sediments are interbedded with them. They differ chemically from later eruptions, being mainly **basalt** and basaltic-**andesite** lavas. Their small outcrop (less than 50 km^2) in a narrow belt across the extreme northern fringe of the district does not do justice to the great activity which produced them. Another exposure is at the foot of Cross Fell. The gap between the outcrops suggests the Eycott Lavas are largely hidden by younger rocks.

The rocks of the Borrowdale Volcanic Group, which succeed the Eycott Group, were formed during the main volcanic episode. They are the real heart of Lakeland, extending from Wasdale and the Duddon valley in the west through Scafell to Helvellyn, High Street and Haweswater in the east. Over 6000 m thickness of these rocks were erupted in 10 million years during the mid-Ordovician. Today they cover an area of 800 km^2.

Detailed examination of these rocks has helped to build a fascinating picture of the type of vulcanism responsible. It resembles that of the Cascade Ranges of the United States where Mount St Helens erupted so spectacularly in 1980. The evidence indicates that these volcanoes erupted in a sub-aerial environment (on dry land). However some of the material seems to have collected in short-lived freshwater lakes, and streams eroded the fresh pile of volcanic material, transporting and reworking its debris.

Two major phases can be distinguished in the Borrowdale Group. The first, in which 2500 m of rock accumulated, was dominated by lava flows with occasional explosive eruptions. There were several vents or centres of activity. Lavas, usually andesitic, flowed across the landscape, probably building relatively low-lying piles of material. The lava flows were quite localized, their thickness, and rates and distances of flow depending on their composition and the local relief. Many broke up and shattered as they flowed. This was because their exposed upper and lower surfaces cooled and solidified, whilst their hot interiors remained liquid and continued to flow. There is also a suggestion that some of the beds are not true lava flows but peperitic sills, formed from lava being forced into wet unconsolidated sediments close to the surface.

Occasional explosive activity threw fine ash into the atmosphere to fall back as **air-fall tuffs**. These materials were particularly susceptible to rain-wash and stream erosion, and many exposures show materials re-deposited by stream action (**volcaniclastic** sediments). Such features are described in Excursion 7 in the area between Ennerdale and Wasdale.

The second phase marked an abrupt change to explosive activity with **ignimbrite** sheets, **pyroclastic surge** and **fall** deposits. Enormous volumes of material were erupted very quickly. These were very violent eruptions, similar to that of Vesuvius in AD 79 which destroyed Pompeii. Explosive eruptions of silica-rich andesite, **dacite** and **rhyolite** magmas threw material high into the atmosphere, where it spread widely before falling back to the ground as an air-fall tuff. Ignimbrites formed when surges of fluidized material flowed across the landscape. These mixtures of solid fragments and gas at 500–600 °C were hot enough to weld together when they finally came to rest, and their sheer weight often flattened the pumice fragments to elongated **fiamme**, giving the rocks a streaky (**eutaxitic**) texture. Such deposits dominate the upper Borrowdale succession.

The present central Lake District is very different from the original Ordovician volcanic terrain. Much has been removed by erosion. Large parts of the original volcano broke away, tilted and sank into the molten volcanic pile, a process known as caldera collapse. The outcrop is much affected by both vertical and horizontal fault movements. The sheer variety of rock types, their complex structures and differing responses to weathering and erosion have produced a remarkably intricate landscape.

The Windermere Group

More than 5000 m of very varied sedimentary materials, the Windermere Group, lie on top of the volcanic rocks. The succession ranges in age from very late Ordovician to end Silurian, (see Table 1). These rocks form the third major belt of the lower Palaeozoic core, extending across southern Lakeland from the Duddon estuary to the Howgill Fells. Generally they form lower fell country than either Borrowdale or Skiddaw Group rocks.

Towards the end of the Ordovician, the Iapetus Ocean had almost closed and Skiddaw Group sediments had been crumpled as the American and European plates converged. The Dent Subgroup (formerly termed the Coniston Limestone) – the lowest sedimentary formation of the Windermere Group – lies above an **unconformity**, an eroded surface cutting across both Borrowdale Volcanic and Skiddaw Group rocks. These two groups of rock must have been uplifted and eroded before the Dent Subgroup was deposited. It outcrops in a 50 km linear strip, rarely over 150 m thick, between Shap and the Duddon estuary. Besides thin limestones suggesting a rich shelf-sea environment, it contains some volcanic materials from the last dying throes of Ordovician volcanic activity.

There was continuous sedimentation throughout the Silurian, and the seas deepened as subsidence occurred. Thick turbidite sequences of sandstones, flagstones, gritstones, mudstones and dark shales were laid down. Most are quite fossiliferous so the sequence is relatively easy to follow. Excursions 3 and 5 visit different parts of the Windermere Group outcrop.

INTRUSIONS

The igneous intrusions are the fourth and very distinctive group of rocks in the main core. They range in size from substantial plutonic bodies like the Eskdale Granite to small **plugs**, **dykes** and **sills**. The Shap, Eskdale and Skiddaw Granites are described in Excurions 2, 7 and 14. Excursion 11 visits the much smaller Armboth Dyke.

The Lake District is an east–west belt of relatively low **gravity anomalies**, with minima over Eskdale, Shap and Skiddaw. This suggests the area is underlain at depth by a large **batholith** of granitic material of relatively low density (which extends westwards under the Isle of Man and east under Weardale and much of County Durham). The exposed granites are parts of the roof of the batholith uncovered by erosion.

The batholith appears to be composite; formed from a series of intrusions related to the volcanic episodes. The earliest event emplaced the Carrock Fell **Gabbro** complex at the same time as the Eycott Volcanic Group. Several minor intrusions followed, such as the Great Cockup **picrite** and the Threlkeld microgranites, all probably associated with the Borrowdale Volcanic Group.

A major phase later in the Ordovician produced the Eskdale Granite which has the largest exposure. Slightly later **plutons** like the Ennerdale **Granophyre** formed at the same time as the very late volcanic outbursts in Coniston Limestone times. Finally even later events in the Lower Devonian produced the Shap and Skiddaw Granites and the mineralizing fluids which penetrated the overlying Skiddaw, Borrowdale and Windermere Group rocks. This is the origin of much of the mineral wealth of the Lake District, in particular the ores of copper, tungsten and iron. A major concealed part of the batholith is also early Devonian in age and underlies part of the northwestern fells. The associated Crummock Water **aureole** extends over 20 km parallel to the Causey Pike fault belt.

The formative phase of Lake District geological history, the first 100 million years, was nearing its climax by the end of Silurian times. The Iapetus Ocean had closed, but the continental collision – the peak of the Caledonian mountain building, which culminated in early Devonian times – was yet to come.

The Caledonian orogeny extended over a long period and took place in distinct phases. In the first phase, which preceded Borrowdale Volcanic Group rocks, Skiddaw Group sediments were uplifted and great thicknesses removed by erosion before the vulcanicity began. There may also have been some crumpling at this stage. A second phase of uplift and doming occurred before sediments of the Dent subgroup were laid down when the deep granitic batholith had began to rise.

The main (Lower Devonian) phase took place after the Iapetus Ocean had been destroyed and the two colliding continents buckled and welded together to form the new Eur-American continent. The effects on relief and structure were far-reaching. The mountain chains were possibly of Himalayan proportions and extended across the southeast of the new continent, including Scandinavia, northwest Britain and the northeast of North America. The rocks were uplifted into a southwest–northeast trending dome. Heat and pressure metamorphosed many of the Skiddaw sediments into slates, and a strong cleavage developed, especially in the volcanic rocks. Major faulting also took place.

The various rock groups responded differently to the earth movements. The relatively weak Skiddaw Group sediments deformed in a complex fashion, whilst most of the volcanic rocks withstood pressure better and now show rather broad open folds with many layers still being almost horizontal. The Windermere Group sediments responded in a variety of ways: thick sandstones and gritstones resisted distortion but intervening fine-grained beds were severely crushed and crumpled.

DEVONIAN AND CARBONIFEROUS

The new Eur-American continent created by the Caledonian orogeny was in desert latitudes in the southern hemisphere (probably around 20°S). Lakeland was part of the mountain chain and was subject to weathering and erosion for most of the Devonian. The Mell Fell **Conglomerate** is the only Lake District deposit of this period. It is a coarse-grained, poorly-sorted rock, probably laid down in a series of **alluvial fans**. It contains Lower Palaeozoic material of Lakeland origin. Today it forms the rounded hills of Great and Little Mell Fell near the lower end of Ullswater.

By Carboniferous times erosion had worn down the Caledonian highlands, allowing shallow seas to extend over the land; and by the end of the Dinantian (Lower Carboniferous) these tropical seas, rich in life, covered the whole of Lakeland, resulting in limestone deposition. Namurian (mid-Carboniferous) **cyclothem** sequences consisting of sandstones, shales and gritstones followed the limestones. Eventually, as the landmass reached equatorial latitudes the landscape became one of tropical delta swamp forests which produced the Coal Measure sequences of the Westphalian.

At the end of the Carboniferous the Hercynian orogeny elevated the area for a second time. Its effects were mild compared to the Caledonian, and the Lower Palaeozoic core and underlying granitic batholith formed a resistant massif. Some gentle folding and moderate faulting occurred. Basins surrounding the Lake District (such as the Vale of Eden) were downwarped, and there was considerable movement along major fault systems to the east along the Pennine edge. Carboniferous beds now dip gently outwards at less than 10° from the central core.

Carboniferous rocks almost completely encircle the Lower Palaeozoic core of the Lake District, forming distinctive terrains. For example weathering and glacial erosion have shaped many Dinantian limestones into **karst** landscapes, whilst Namurian strata in the extreme north and southeast give rise to scarp and vale topography akin to the Pennines. In West Cumbria the Coal Measures underlie the coastal strip between Whitehaven and Maryport. Excursions 1, 4, 15 and 18 visit contrasting areas of the Carboniferous outcrop.

PERMIAN AND TRIASSIC

Permo-Triassic rocks outcrop in the Vale of Eden, around Carlisle, along the West Cumbrian coast south of Whitehaven and on the edge of Morecambe Bay. Excursions 8 and 16 visit some of these areas. The rocks are mainly red beds deposited in desert conditions. Continuing continental drift had moved the Lake District north into the latitudes of Northern Hemisphere deserts. The exposed dome of Carboniferous sediments was being eroded off the Lower Palaeozoic core and thick deposits were being laid down in the surrounding basins. The mountain core was being buried once again.

Conditions were similar to those in the Arabian Peninsula today. It was an arid environment, with northeast trade winds moving sand and building dunes. The earliest deposits were **breccias** (**Brockrams**), formed as screes and alluvial fans on the edges of Lakeland. The overlying and interbedded Penrith Sandstone is a sand-sea deposit. **Evaporite** deposits in the higher sequences (mainly **gypsum** and **anhydrite**) suggest conditions in the Upper Permian were similar to those in parts of today's very saline Persian Gulf.

What happened in our area in the 200 million years of geological history since the Triassic is largely guesswork because the region has hardly any deposits from these times. A very small patch of Jurassic sediments lies on the Triassic Plain west of Carlisle. The nearest Cretaceous rocks are in Northern Ireland and there are no Tertiary deposits. Material from all these periods may have been laid down over the Lake District and later removed by erosion, but there is no direct evidence of this. However the events of the late Tertiary and especially of the Quaternary are essential to our story.

TERTIARY

According to the orthodox view of Tertiary events, the generally radial drainage pattern of today was **superimposed** on the region from an earlier pattern of drainage formed on the dome of pre-Triassic rocks. This dome was supposedly uplifted in the third great period of mountain building (the Alpine orogeny) during the late Tertiary. There is doubt about all three ideas. The radial drainage pattern may be partly explained by structural control and by later glacial erosion. Superimposition can only be proved if the other two ideas are accepted. The effect of the Alpine earth movements on the Lake District is debatable. Lakeland is far from the centre of activity, the Alpine areas of Southern Europe, and how much gentle doming of the Lake District took place then is uncertain (though we know that some movement occurred, particularly along old fault lines). The important and incontrovertible truth is that the Lower Palaeozoic core of the Lakeland fells stood high above the surrounding lowlands by late Tertiary times. The 'Caledonian Mountains' had reasserted themselves. Since then, they have been etched by weathering and erosion for as much as 50 million years.

QUATERNARY

The effects of events in the Quaternary, the last 1.8 million years, are so fresh in the Lakeland landscape that they are often overemphasised. This was a period of worldwide climatic change. Britain oscillated between fully glacial and warmer interglacial conditions, with at least 11 and possibly 16 cold phases. Like other uplands, the Lake District shows little evidence of the early glacial phases. Only traces of the last major glacial, the late Devensian (30 000–10 000 BP, i.e. before present) remain fresh. An ice sheet covered the whole area, the highest summits being several hundred metres below its surface. The exact mechanisms by which glaciers erode rock are not altogether clear, but the ice sheet overdeepened many of the main valleys, creating lake basins, 'roughened up' landscapes underlain by igneous rock and excavated **corrie** basins in the heads of upland valleys. Although the Lake District is spectacular and rugged by British standards it is not a classic glaciated landscape like the Alps.

The effects of deposition in the Pleistocene are far clearer. Unconsolidated deposits of glacial **till**, **moraines**, **drumlins**, sands and gravels mantle many valley floors and cover many of the surrounding lowlands. The sediments in the lake basins have allowed detailed stratigraphies to be worked out for the Lake District and correlations to be made with other European areas.

The effects of a minor late glacial phase, the Loch Lomond **Stadial**, are very clear. Cold conditions lasted for less than 1000 years (from about 11 000–10 000 BP), leading to corrie and upland glaciers re-establishing themselves at higher levels, especially in the central fells.

Excursions 10, 12 and 13 describe glacial landforms and Quaternary deposits in the area.

This introductory chapter has been brisk, describing 500 million years of earth history in about 4000 words. The excursion chapters which follow are case studies of specific areas and themes. The books listed under Further Reading (p. 146) will allow the curious reader to delve into many fascinating arguments about the origins of the Lake District, an incomparably beautiful and varied region.

1 · Lower Carboniferous rocks near Orton, east of Shap

Alan Day *formerly Field Secretary, Westmorland Geological Society*

PURPOSE

To trace the Carboniferous succession: from the continental rocks at the base, up to the limestones of a carbonate shelf; to look at the richly varied fossils; and to appreciate how geological processes have affected landscape development.

PRACTICAL DETAILS

One day, best taken as two half days. In Part 1 (viewing the basal rocks west and south of Orton) walking is minimal but transport is essential. Please park carefully on the narrow lanes to avoid causing inconvenience, especially to farm vehicles. The map (Figure 1.2) shows the route and locations visited in this Part. In Part 2 there is a 4 km walk, with a short uphill section, to view some of the upper limestones east of Orton. The excursion starts from Orton (see Figure 1.1). Roads are narrow but suitable for cars.

Toilet facilities are available in Orton village near the central car park, as are shops, a restaurant and a pub. Figure 1.1 is a general map of the area covered during the excursion. Some of the ground walked is rough exposed fellside so appropriate clothing and suitable strong footwear are recommended.

OS MAP: 1:50 000, Sheet 91

GEOLOGICAL SETTING

The quiet village of Orton stands on the dip slope of the lower of two prominent escarpments of Lower Carboniferous rocks. The upper escarpment rises to the north and northeast above the village, showing

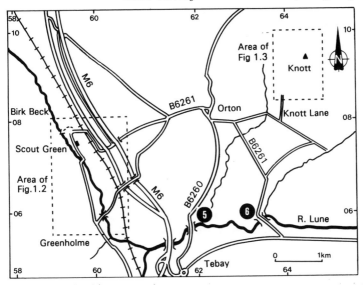

Figure 1.1 The Orton and Tebay areas, showing Locations 5 and 6.

step topography often associated with horizontal or nearly horizontally bedded limestones and sandstones.

A regional dip of 5–10° northeast brings most of the succession to
the surface, but soil and glacial drift obscure some sections. A major
unconformity is exposed within the area along Birk Beck. It is worth
the short diversion outside the area to visit the section in Wasdale
Beck (578095) near Shap Wells Hotel, where gently dipping basal
Carboniferous **conglomerates**, shales and sandstones overlie steeply
dipping Silurian mudstones (see Excursion 2).

As the sea encroached over an eroded land surface of moderate relief
it filled existing hollows with varying thicknesses of sandstones and
conglomerates, followed by limestones and shales as sea levels rose.
The underlying Silurian rocks are about 50 **Ma** older than the basal
Carboniferous rocks. This marine inundation originally came from
the east along the Ravenstonedale Trough, but the whole of what is
now the Lake District was probably under water when the limestones
on the top of Orton Scar were deposited.

The landscape has been much modified by glaciation and river
action. **Erratics** of the Borrowdale Volcanic Group, Shap Granite and
Silurian rocks are common. Directions of ice flow in the area can be
established by tracing these erratics back to their outcrops.

EXCURSION DETAILS

Part 1 (see Figure 1.2)

Drive west of Orton along the B6261, turning at the first junction along the minor road signposted to Scout Green. Stop at the viewpoint near Sproatgill Farm (603076), just before the M6. The well-drained upper limestone scarp rises to the north. To the west the lower limestone scarp gives way to the marshy valley of Birk Beck underlain by sandstones and conglomerates. The rounded hills composed of Silurian rocks of the Windermere Group rise beyond the river, with the Shap Granite and its prominent quarry to the northwest. Drive under the M6 bridges.

Location 1 (599075) is by the roadside. Just northeast of it, 30 m from a bridge, a grey-green conglomerate outcrops. Look for **clasts** of vein quartz, volcanic rocks, **greywackes** and **slates** within a coarse sandy

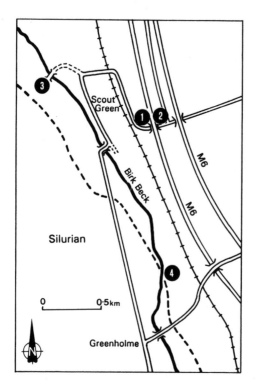

Figure 1.2 The Orton area with Locations 1–4.

matrix. Pink orthoclase **phenocrysts** from the Shap Granite can also be seen in this poorly sorted conglomerate whose clasts are derived from nearby outcrops to the north and northwest. The grey-green colour suggests **chloritization** in a marine environment.

Location 2 (600075) is between the M6 bridges. Marine bivalves occur in mudstones that are higher in the stratigraphic succession than the conglomerate. Drive under the railway and park halfway down the hill near the sharp left-hand bend. Walk along the track to the right to Shepherd's Bridge over Birk Beck.

Location 3 (590077) is by this bridge. Look for **tabular** and **trough cross-bedded**, poorly cemented sandstones and thin layers of conglomerate in the river bank. The redness of the sandstone shows that the iron present was oxidized in subaerial conditions. The cross-bedding, red colours and alternating fine and coarse layers suggest that a **braided** stream deposited its load of angular fragments of local rocks in semi-arid conditions.

Drive south past Scout Green farm to Greenholme, turn left across Birk Beck and park by the third gate on the left 200 m up the hill at an inset of the road wall. Cut diagonally across the field to the river bank (having obtained permission from Bridge End Farm).

Location 4 (599061) is on the river bank *which can be slippery and very wet after heavy rain*. Notice the steeply dipping and **cleaved** Silurian slates in the river bed and a few metres upstream a thick bed of well-rounded cobbles lying unconformably above the Silurian slates and outcropping in a low cliff on the river bank. The cobbles are locally derived Silurian mudstones and shales – virtually one rock type with little matrix. This is a well-sorted conglomerate probably deposited by an early Carboniferous river flood. The **imbricate** fabric of the conglomerate shows the direction of stream flow. The particle size in the beds fines upwards which shows that the stream current slackened. Return to Orton and proceed south along the B6260.

Location 5 (619056) is Tebay Bridge over the River Lune. Park south of the bridge and go to the river bank through the gate and over the stile. Notice the sandstone in the river bed, particularly detached blocks on the **point bar**. Fine mud flakes in the coarse sandstones are **rip-up** clasts which accumulated to form a mud flake conglomerate. At low water, mud and silt were deposited, hardening subaerially later. Flash floods broke up these hardened layers, incorporating the mud flakes within the sands they eventually deposited. Drive to the roundabout at Tebay, turn left along the A685 and left again at a petrol station along the B6261.

Location 6 (635058) is Raisgill Hall Bridge. Look at the beds on the north bank, west of the bridge. Sandy limestone and blue-grey shale are followed here by purer limestones, indicating deeper, clearer water. We now leave the lower subaerially deposited and transition beds.

Part 2 (see Figure 1.3)

Drive to Knott Lane, parking on the roadside at (639079), on the dip slope of the poorly exposed lowest limestones. Walk along Knott Lane, passing Gamelands, a stone circle in a field to the right. The rise in Knott Lane is due to the unexposed Ashfell sandstone. Go through the gate near the lime kiln on to the open fell. The upper escarpment is mainly Ashfell Limestone (Holkerian stage), Potts Beck and Knipe Scar Limestones (both Asbian stage).

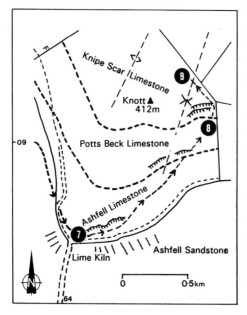

Figure 1.3 The Orton Scar area, rock types and Locations 7–9.

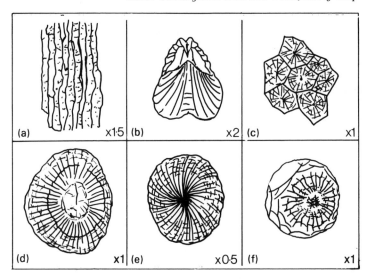

Figure 1.4 Lower Carboniferous fossils: (a) *Syringopora*;
(b) *Davidsonina carbonaria*; (c) *Lithostrotion sp.*; (d) *Dibunophyllum*;
(e) *Palaeosmilia*; (f) *Axophyllum*.

Location 7 (641085) is a small quarry in basal Ashfell limestone immediately opposite the gate. This marks the beginning of a major marine transgression. Its beds are massive and cross-bedded, with fossils abraded and broken by strong currents during its deposition. Walk diagonally uphill to the right for about 200 m to the group of small quarries which are slightly higher in the succession and clearly visible from Knott Lane. These limestones have a rich fauna, fossils often being beautifully etched out on quarry faces. Species of the **tabulate** coral *Syringopora* with its closely spaced tubes (Figure 1.4a) and the brachiopod *Linoprotonia* dominate some horizons. Other fossils present include the brachiopod *Davidsonina carbonaria* with its distinctive Y-shaped outline (Figure 1.4b) and the compound **rugose** coral *Lithostrotion* (Figure 1.4c). Notice the chert nodules, a form of silica whose origin is still being debated.

Continue uphill to the northeast, crossing limestone bands, some of which contain the fossil coral *Chaetetes*, looking rather like irregular dark balls of lichen on the light grey rock. Further uphill (at about 644087), a very different limestone outcrops. This is more rubbly, forming knobbly lumps in which bedding planes are indistinct, and is the lower boundary of the Potts Limestone of Asbian age. Notice how the limestone crags alternate with flatter grassy areas underlain by sandstones and shales. Continue in the same direction towards the wall.

Location 8 (648092) is where the Knipe Scar Limestone appears by the wall. Locally this is part of the Great Scar Limestone, the rock which forms most of the limestone pavement in the Western Pennines. This limestone is crowded with fossil corals, mainly solitary varieties including species of *Dibunophyllum* (Figure 1.4d), *Palaeosmilia* (Figure 1.4e) and *Axophyllum* (Figure 1.4f). Specimens of the large brachiopod *Gigantoproductus* can also be found. The rubbly limestone continues with occasional shale partings as we follow the wall uphill to where it turns northwest. Head west for 120 m to the triangulation point (421 m at 646092) from which there is a fine view of the ground we have crossed. Walk 200 m north to return to the wall.

Location 9 (647094) is where the wall turns northwest. Just to the north, limestone pavement is exposed in a broad asymmetric syncline trending and plunging north-northeast. Follow the wall over the limestones to reach the top of the western limb, which is also the crest of the complementary anticline. Continue along the wall past the beautifully preserved limestone pavement with its **clints** and **grykes** until you can turn left to the south and southwest, preferably along the grassy rake joining the track back to the gate and Knott Lane.

2 · The Shap Granite

Eric Skipsey *formerly of the Open University*

PURPOSE

To examine the Shap Granite and the associated metamorphism of surrounding rocks; to appreciate the **unconformity** at Shap Wells and how it helps to date the granite; and to look at folding in Silurian rocks.

PRACTICAL DETAILS

A one-day excursion. Transport between locations is needed. Appropriate windproof clothing and suitable strong footwear are essential. Safety helmets must be worn at the quarry.

The locations are near the A6 road, 2 km south of Shap village, with adequate parking nearby. There are public toilets and cafés in Shap village and the Shap Wells Hotel provides excellent amenities.

Only a limited number of parties are allowed to visit the Shap Granite Quarry so early application is recommended. Write, enclosing a stamped addressed envelope, to: Shap Granite Quarry Ltd, Shap, Penrith, Cumbria CA10 3QQ. The company requires all parties to take out adequate insurance cover. Party leaders should report to the offices at the entrance to the Shap Concrete Products works before going to the quarry. There is no access to the Blue Quarry but specimens of intrusive and country rocks are on display at the Granite Quarry.

Permission to visit Wasdale Head Farm and the granite contact (Locations 2, 4 and 5) should be obtained from the Lowther Estate Office, Lowther, Penrith, CA11 2HG (Tel: 09312 392). Please also inform the farmer, Mr Peter Allen, Grange House Farm, Bampton, Penrith (Tel: 09313 236). Permission may be refused during the shooting season between August and December.

OS MAPS: 1:25 000 Outdoor Leisure Maps, The English Lakes, North Eastern and South Eastern areas

             1:50 000 Sheets 90 (Locations 1–4) and 91 (Locations 5 and 6)

BGS MAP: 1:250 000

GEOLOGICAL SETTING

The Shap Granite is one of the best-known and most distinctive rock types in Northern England, with its coarse texture and large pink crystals or **megacrysts**. Although the Shap Granite outcrop is small (5.5 km^2), geophysical studies show it to be a steep-sided intrusion with a subsurface extension to the northwest. The intrusion and broad **metasomatic aureole** occur at the junction between Borrowdale Volcanic Group rocks and the Windermere Group to the south. It is later than the end-Silurian deformation which folded the country rocks and has been dated to 393+/−10 Ma, the beginning of Devonian times. Figure 2.1 shows the main rock formations of the area and the locations visited.

EXCURSION DETAILS

Location 1 (558084) is Shap Granite Quarry. The quarry provides excellent exposures but keep well away from all faces and machinery. Look for the following features.

There is a definite joint pattern. The three main systems, one almost horizontal and two near vertical, produce almost rectangular blocks.

The main features of the granite are the megacrysts and its division into darker and lighter varieties. The megacrysts are pink **orthoclase feldspars** with good rectangular shapes and **twinning** parallel to the long axes of the crystals. The fine groundmass consists of quartz, **biotite**, orthoclase and white **plagioclase** feldspar. Colour variations are probably due to secondary **hematite** which formed from the decomposition of biotite.

There are various dark patches (**enclaves**) in the granite. The photograph (Figure 2.2) illustrates one of these. They can be angular or rounded, and may have either sharp or fuzzy boundaries with the normal granite. They usually contain pink megacrysts, which are less frequent and more rounded than in the normal granite. The enclaves are thought to be either portions of a more basic, deeper intrusion caught in the emplacement of the granite, or blocks of the surrounding lavas incompletely assimilated into the granitic magma. See if you can identify these enclaves.

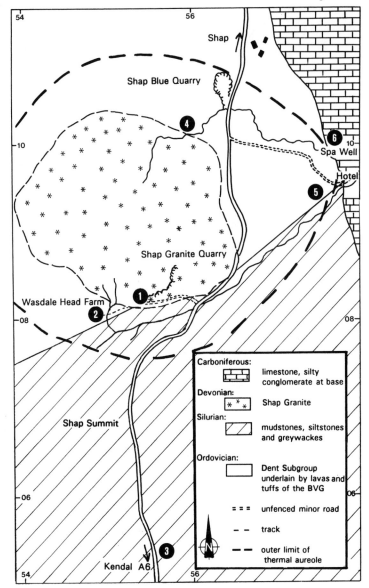

Figure 2.1 The Shap Granite and surrounding strata.

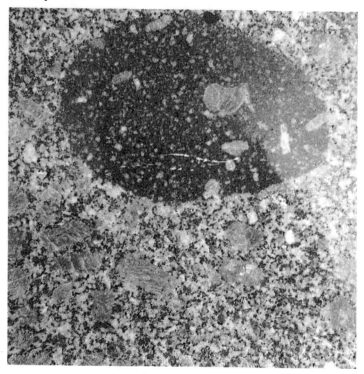

Figure 2.2 Polished section showing megacrysts and a dark enclave in the Shap granite. *Photo*: E. Skipsey

The granite has been altered and extensively mineralized. Look for fine-grained pink veins, often with quartz-rich centres. These are **aplite** veins, formed by **hydrothermal** fluids leaching feldspars from the granite. Notice mineral coatings on joint faces. The following minerals may be present: hematite, **molybdenite, pyrite, chalcopyrite, fluorite, barite, epidote**, calcite and quartz. Much 'rotting' of feldspars occurs along some major joints, forming bands of soft impure **kaolinite**.

There are large blocks of the Borrowdale Volcanic Group on display in the granite quarry. These darker rocks were quarried from the Shap Blue Quarry and they have been altered both by earlier thermal metamorphism and metasomatism caused by the granite to the south. Much of the original rock was fine-grained **vesicular andesite**. Many former vesicles have become green feathery masses of

amphiboles as a result of alteration. Elsewhere quartz and calcite filled vesicles to form amygdales (later infills) before the granite was intruded. Fluids from the granite have resulted in numerous mineral veins. The more common minerals include quartz, pyrite, calcite, hematite, red-brown **garnets** and yellow-green epidote.

Location 2 (549081), the site of Wasdale Head Farm, shows the metamorphic aureole.

Join the track below the spoil heaps in the lower part of the granite quarry and follow it for almost 1 km to the site of Wasdale Head Farm. There are several small crags above the path about 100 m beyond the site. The lower exposures of greyish-white granular rocks are thermally metamorphosed Dent Subgroup sediments (formerly termed Coniston Limestone). Immediately above are pink and grey fine-grained **flow-banded rhyolitic** lavas dipping beneath the limestones. The granite contact is best seen in stream gullies just north of the farm.

Location 3 (555055) shows folded Silurian strata on Shap Fell summit. This is a fine roadside section of strongly folded Silurian strata a few hundred metres south of the summit. The grass verges give access to the exposures and there are laybys on either side of the road at the summit. *Beware of fast traffic.*

The sediments belong to a sequence transitional between the Coniston Subgroup (formerly Coniston Grit) and the Bannisdale Formation (formerly Bannisdale Slate) of the Silurian Period (see Table 2, p. 3). They consist of well-**cleaved** mudstones (**laminated** in places), less well-cleaved siltstones and **greywackes** almost without cleavage. This section is beyond the metamorphic aureole of the granite. In parts of the section the sediments dip uniformly and steeply to the south. Intervening areas have tightly folded anticlines and synclines with cleavage generally parallel to fold axes. The photograph (Figure 2.3) illustrates these. This is a good place to study fold structures such as cleavage and **tension gashes**, and sedimentary structures on bedding planes such as **sole marks**, **load casts** and **flute marks**.

Location 4 (562101) is the granite contact. *Please do not hammer here.*

Leave the A6 at the Shap Blue Quarry entrance and follow the track south beside the plantation for about 400 m to a junction by a shed. Some 20 m south of this is a large granite block with a thick quartz stringer. Take the right-hand track to a bridge near a gate.

Figure 2.3 Folded Silurian greywacke in roadside cutting on the A6, Shap Fell. *Photo*: E. Skipsey

Tongues and veins of pink granite can be seen penetrating the country rock in the stream bed below the bridge, proving that the granite is intrusive. With its strings of deformed amygdales the country rock resembles the andesite on display at the Shap Granite Quarry but it has been extensively recrystallized to become a hard, fine-grained **hornfels**. There is little sign that the granite has chilled margins – it is coarse-grained right up to its contacts with aplite veins. Notice the detached, angular fragments of andesite split off by granite injected along cracks.

Location 5 (578095) shows the Shap Wells unconformity. Take the A6 south from the Shap Blue Quarry entrance and turn left down the road signposted 'Shap Wells Hotel'. Ask permission at the hotel to use the large car park.

The section is in the bed and banks of Wasdale Beck upstream from the hotel. *Please do not hammer.* Walk to the waterfall to look at the siltstones and greywackes. Their hard splintery nature results from slight baking by the nearby Shap Granite. Look for faint cross-laminations in the Silurian strata which indicate the direction of dip. This is fairly steeply southeast, at right angles to the roughly northeast–southwest regional strike of the Lower Palaeozoic rocks.

Look at the right bank of the stream below the waterfall. Weakly consolidated greenish and reddish gravels and sandstones dipping gently east-southeast overlie and truncate steeply dipping Silurian beds. This is an unconformity, a time gap, indicated by changes in the direction and amount of dip of the bedding planes above and below the erosion surface. The strata above the unconformity pass up into red shales and sandstones which, being unfossiliferous, are difficult to date. These outcrop downstream nearer the hotel. The red beds are overlain, apparently conformably, by fossiliferous limestones of Lower Carboniferous age exposed along the M6 east of Shap Wells. The red beds must therefore be of very early Carboniferous age.

You can find abundant orthoclase crystals derived from the Shap Granite in the red beds. It follows that these beds could only have accumulated after the granite had been exposed by erosion very early in Carboniferous times.

Location 6 (579096) is the Blea Beck section at Shap Wells. Follow the footpath 300 m from the old house at the northwest corner of the hotel car park through the woods along Blea Beck past Spa Well. Southeast dipping Dent Subgroup rocks – impure limestones, mudstones and volcanic ashes – are exposed in the stream bed. A band of rhyolite forms a waterfall. The unconformity is exposed in the stream bed with Carboniferous sandstones burying the Ordovician surface.

3 · Windermere Group rocks around Tarn Hows

John Gunner *formerly Geology Tutor at Brathay Field Studies Centre*

PURPOSE

To examine the lower part of the Windermere Group succession between the northern ends of Lakes Windermere and Coniston.

PRACTICAL DETAILS

This is a one-day anticlockwise circuit along minor roads between Ambleside and Coniston, starting from either Location 1 or Location 2. There are no restrictions on access. Those travelling by car or minibus have only short distances to walk, but coach passengers will need to walk about 4 km from Hawkshead Hill to Tarn Hows and back. Some of the ground is rough and wet, so suitable strong footwear is necessary. There are shops, public toilets and a range of services in Ambleside, Hawkshead and Coniston. You will find information about parking under 'Excursion Details' below.

OS MAPS: 1:50 000 Sheets 90 and 97
1:63 360 (One Inch), Touring Map No 3, The English Lake District
1:25 000 Outdoor Leisure Map, The English Lakes, South Eastern area

GEOLOGICAL SETTING

Tarn Hows lies at the junction of the Upper Ordovician Borrowdale Volcanic Group (BVG) and the overlying Ordovician and Silurian Windermere Group, which are almost entirely sedimentary rocks deposited near the southern margins of the **Iapetus** Ocean as it closed.

26

Their deposition was preceded by uplift and deep erosion of the underlying volcanic rocks producing an **unconformity**. Shelf-sea conditions followed with the deposition of the Dent Subgroup (formerly termed the Coniston Limestone Formation) rich in benthonic (bottom-dwelling) fossils. Towards the end of this episode the sea deepened and overlying mudstones and **greywackes** were deposited in the narrow trough which was all that remained of the Iapetus Ocean.

Windermere Group rocks dip to the south or southeast and their outcrops run northeast to southwest. Many north–south trending faults cut across these outcrops. Large natural exposures are rare so most of the locations visited are old quarries. Figure 3.1 shows the chief geological features and the locations visited. Table 3.1 shows the succession in the area, giving the new lithostratigraphic terms and their old equivalents.

EXCURSION DETAILS

Leave Ambleside along the A593 Coniston road. In Clappersgate turn left along the B5286 towards Hawkshead. After 1.5 km turn right along the road signposted Tarn Hows and Coniston. Park 250 m further on by the roadside near a gate and stile on the left. Walk up the asphalt track for 200 m and take the right fork into the main quarry. Figure 3.2 shows our route and locates the features described in Brathay Quarries.

Location 1 (357016) is Brathay Quarries in the Brathay Formation (formerly termed the Brathay Flags). This and many smaller quarries to the northeast were worked for building stone, in some cases until the mid-twentieth century. Many Victorian buildings in Ambleside, including Gilbert Scott's Parish Church, are faced with the distinctive blue-black Brathay Flags with their characteristic **pyrite**-flecked joint planes.

The main quarry is at least 10 m deep, so *be careful!* We start to its west at **1** on Figure 3.2, the base of a short ramp 20 m south of a derelict hut, and walk in an anti-clockwise direction. The rocks here are massive mudstones with laminae (thin layers, here 0.5 to 5 mm thick) of alternating dark claystones and paler siltstones. There are a few small **flame structures** which penetrate up to 1 cm into overlying layers.

An overgrown spoil heap, 30 m south of the derelict hut, has a typical flagstone slab, 5 m long and 30 cm thick, like those used as

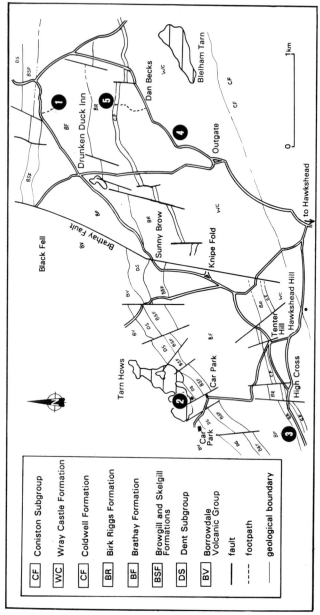

Figure 3.1 Geological sketch map of Windermere Group rocks in the area between Tarn Hows and Brathay Quarries. (Based on O'Connor, B. (1969) *Structure and Sedimentation in part of the Ordovician and Silurian of the Central Southern Lake District*, unpublished M.Sc. Thesis, Liverpool University.)

OLD NAMES	NEW NAMES	
Coniston Grit Formation	**Coniston Subgroup**	
Upper ⎫	**Wray Castle Formation** ⎫	
Middle ⎬ Coldwell Beds	**Coldwell Formation** ⎬ **Tranearth**	
Lower ⎭	**Birk Riggs Formation** ⎭ **Subgroup**	
Brathay Flags	**Brathay Formation**	
Browgill Beds	**Browgill Formation** ⎫ **Stockdale**	
Skelgill Beds	**Skelgill Formation** ⎭ **Subgroup**	
Coniston Limestone Formation	**Dent Subgroup**	
Borrowdale Volcanic Group	**Borrowdale Volcanic Group**	

Table 3.1 The Windermere Group succession around Tarn Hows showing both old and new lithostratigraphic names.

floors for local buildings since at least the seventeenth century. Brathay Church (362033) contains fine examples.

Scramble a short distance through scrub to the southwest corner of the quarry (**2** on Figure 3.2). At about 5 m above the water there are massive mudstones with extremely fine laminae. *Take care!* Return to the top of the main quarry face and continue around its south side. Near the southwest corner a mudstone exposure shows well-developed vertical **cleavage** which strikes northeast.

Continue through scrub to the east side of the main quarry (**3** on Figure 3.2) and notice how the rocks on the opposite face dip south. On top of an overgrown ramp are many quarried blocks of mudstone, often bounded by bedding and joint surfaces intersecting at 60° to 80°. Sheets of calcite and quartz coat the bedding surfaces of several blocks near **3**. Some show small-scale drag-folding where adjacent beds have slipped over each other. The spoil heaps east of the main quarry show other examples of Brathay Formation features.

Drive southwest up the hill from Location 1. From near the Drunken Duck Hotel, notice Black Fell, an upfaulted mass of BVG rocks, at the foot of which is the Brathay Fault, whose movement was partly **strike-slip**.

Continue southwestwards past Sunny Brow, where the road follows the fault line for about 1 km, to Tenter Hill. Turn right by a guest house and go up the steep hill to Tarn Hows. Coach passengers should

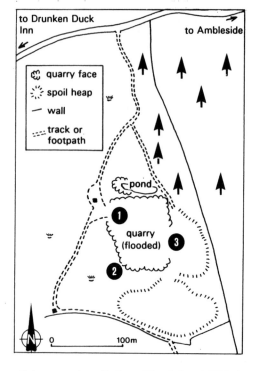

Figure 3.2 A sketch map of Brathay Quarries, showing the localities visited.

alight at and walk from Hawkshead Hill (337988). Other vehicles must approach Tarn Hows from the southeast as the road to the southwest is for outgoing traffic only. There are two car parks: a large western one, where a fee is charged during the season, and a smaller eastern one for disabled people.

Location 2 (330997) is Tarn Hows where the succession from the Borrowdale Volcanic Group up to the Browgill Formation is exposed.

A dam at the southwest corner has formed one lake from several small tarns. This is National Trust property. *Please do not hammer rock exposures.*

A fault block forms much of the land southeast of the tarn, where there is a discontinuous section of most of the Dent Subgroup (formerly the Coniston Limestone). Figure 3.3 shows this succession.

Examine the outcrops, starting 50 m from the lake shore, where a stream descending from the eastern car park crosses the track near a gate. Just west of the track is a **roche moutonnée** of grey-green

andesite with **pyroxene** crystals. This is the top of the enormous pile of the BVG that forms the mountains to the west.

Sedimentary rocks of the Windermere Group, which rest unconformably on the BVG, are tilted here to the southeast and form the escarpment southeast of the track. Cliffs and benches mark the outcrops of more and less resistant beds. The first steep slope east of the track has exposures of tough greenish quartz-veined rocks which weather brown. Initially these may appear to be igneous rocks, but since there are rounded pebbles in some of the lower outcrops the rocks must be sedimentary. They are **conglomerates** and sandstones but resemble the andesite in colour and mineral content because they were derived from volcanic debris and were deposited on the eroded surface of the 'Borrowdale' volcano. Above the basal 3 m of these conglomerates and sandstones, scattered outcrops of sandstone extend up to the first bench.

In the next cliff are limestones and interbedded mudstones. Their lowest exposed bed, a dark grey mudstone with cleavage striking east-northeast, crops out a few metres above a spring near the southern end of the bench. The limestones in this cliff are pale grey. Some are fossiliferous, some nodular, some solution-pitted and some cleaved.

The northeast-trending marshy gully just east of the cliff top may be fault-guided. The dark grey, cleaved and finely laminated beds southeast of the gully contain fossil fragments and are near the top of the Dent Subgroup succession.

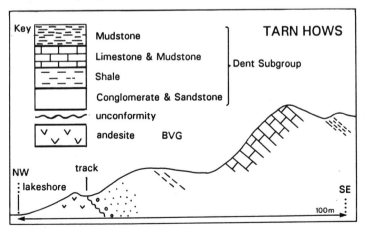

Figure 3.3 A sketch cross-section of the rocks southeast of Tarn Hows.

The small eastern car park contains exposures of the Browgill Formation: pale grey, cleaved, unlaminated mudstones. The tops of the outcrops slope uniformly southeast and are probably bedding planes.

Return from Tarn Hows to Tenter Hill, turn right and proceed to High Cross, where you turn right again to High Cross Plantation Quarry which is 400 m further. Cars and minibuses may be parked here.

Location 3 (328985) is High Cross Plantation Quarry where rocks of the Brathay and Birk Riggs (formerly Lower Coldwell) Formations are exposed.

The quarry contains continuous sequences of the uppermost Brathay Formation and the basal parts of the Birks Riggs Formation. **Turbidite** structures are common and there are good examples of concentric folding and the associated intersections of bedding and cleavage.

The Brathay Formation outcrop occupies the northwest of the quarry, its features resembling those in Brathay Quarries. The large slabs contain buff siltstone laminae, **ripple-drift cross-bedding** and concretions. On the west end of a huge slab directly under an oak tree are **prod marks**, caused by the impact of objects carried by bottom currents along a muddy sea floor. A small fault with **fault gouge** is exposed at the northern corner.

Walk clockwise around the bottom of the face. Halfway along the northeastern face, paler beds – greywacke sandstones of the Birk Riggs Formation – overlie darker Brathay Formation mudstones. These are proximal turbidites, deposited in the middle of submarine fans emerging from the continental slope on to the deep sea floor. Many beds are **graded**. Their muddy tops are cleaved but not their sandy bases. Some bed surfaces have **sole marks**. Load and flame structures are well developed in a 1 m thick bed just south of the eastern corner. Prod and **flute marks** are common here on the underside of beds. *No hammering please!*

There is a small exposure of Coniston Subgroup rocks (formerly Coniston Grits) in a field by the road under a holly tree 70 m southwest of the entry to Thompson Ground Farm (342986). Please seek permission to visit this and to park by the farm from the tenant at Belle Green Farm, Near Sawrey, Ambleside (Tel: 05394 36200).

Descend Hawkshead Hill and turn left past the sawmill at the bottom. Continue along the B5286 for about 500 m beyond Outgate to a prominent rockface on the roadside by a right-hand bend. There is ample parking.

Location 4 (356003), on the Outgate-Ambleside roadside shows Wray Castle Formation (formerly Upper Coldwell) rocks.

A sequence of massive greywackes, dipping gently southeast, crops out here. Many beds are about 1 m thick with mud to sand-size grains. Some beds show ripple-drift cross-bedding, capped by plane (near-horizontal) laminations with uniform mudstones above. The structures suggest these rocks are distal turbidites, deposited at the outer edges of submarine fans on the deep sea floor. **Slickensides** occur on some bedding planes at the north end of the exposure. These are parallel to the dip, suggesting movements between adjacent beds during folding.

From Location 4 follow the road north for 500 m to the Dan Becks entry where there is limited parking east of the road. Walk back a short distance to follow the public footpath north for 300 m along a winding forest track. The disused quarry is east of this path.

Location 5 (359010), Coldwell Quarry, shows outcrops of the Coldwell Formation (formerly Middle Coldwell Beds).

This quarry is flooded, but there is plenty of rock in spoil heaps and exposures on either side of the entrance. The rocks are massive, blue-grey, muddy limestones and calcareous siltstones which dip south. They belong to the Coldwell Formation, the absence of laminations distinguishing them from the Wray Castle and Birk Riggs Formation rocks above and below.

The Coldwell Formation is relatively resistant, forming an up-standing ridge. Quarries and lime kilns are common along its outcrop.

4 · The Carboniferous Limestones of Low Furness

David Kelly *Excursion Secretary, Cumberland Geological Society*

PURPOSE

To investigate the Carboniferous Limestone sequence in Low Furness and its iron ores; and to appreciate how rock type and structure affect the landscape.

PRACTICAL DETAILS

The excursion is in two parts, each requiring a half day. Part 1 is on Birkrigg Common, 4 km south of Ulverston, on open land with easy access and parking. Part 2 is in the Plumpton area, 3 km east of Ulverston, with ample parking, public toilets and a pub. Access is by public footpaths and along the foreshore, rarely covered even at high tide. Permission is needed to visit Locations 9 and 10, and details are given in the itinerary. Ulverston has shops, public toilets and refreshment facilities. Private transport is essential unless you walk from Ulverston. Appropriate clothing and suitable, strong footwear are recommended.

OS MAPS: 1:50 000 Sheet 96
               1:25 000 Sheets SD 27, Barrow in Furness (North), and SD 37, Grange over Sands

BGS MAP: 1:25 000, Classical areas of British Geology series, Dalton in Furness

GEOLOGICAL SETTING

The Lake District is partly surrounded by outcrops of Lower Carboniferous rocks dipping gently away from the central mountain

Formation	Thickness	Characteristics	Stage	Coral-brachiopod zone
GLEASTON FORMATION	200 m	Dark limestones shales & sandstones	Brigantian	D_2
URSWICK LIMESTONE	150 m	Limestones: pale grey, well-bedded joints widely spaced, pseudobrecciated	Asbian	D_1
PARK LIMESTONE	120 m	Limestones: pale grey, medium grained, massive, many joints, weather to scree	Holkerian	S_2
DALTON BEDS	120 m	Limestones: dark-medium grey, medium-grained, shale partings, lower part well-bedded	Arundian	C_2S_1
RED HILL OOLITE	60 m	Limestones: pale grey, well-sorted grains & pellets, massive	Arundian	C_2S_1
MARTIN LIMESTONE	50 m	Limestones: medium grey, fine–medium grains, well-bedded, shale partings	Chadian	C_2S_1 C_1
BASEMENT BEDS	5 m–250 m	Red conglomerates, sandstones, shales, thin limestones	Courceyan	

Table 4.1 The Lower Carboniferous Formations of Low Furness. (Based on Rose and Dunham (1977) Geology and Hematite Deposits of South Cumbria, *Econ. Mem. Geol. Survey*, Sheet 58.)

core. The Furness succession has several lithological formations, five dominated by limestones (see Table 4.1), four of which we visit in this excursion.

These limestones were deposited in warm, clear, shallow seas as Britain drifted northwards through tropical latitudes. Their varying character is due to changes in depositional conditions, particularly in water depth, wave and/or current action and the amount of muddy sediment carried by streams from the landmass to the northwest. Water depth may have fluctuated in cycles: phases of increasing depth producing pale, clear limestones; those of decreasing depth giving rise to dark, muddy limestones, **dolomites** and shales. Fossil specimens should be collected only from loose debris. Excellent examples of corals and brachiopods can be seen on rock faces. *No hammering, please!*

The regional dip is to the southeast or east-southeast at 10–15°, except in the gentle syncline running through Urswick and Gleaston. Faults, mainly trending northwest–southeast and west-northwest–east-southeast, split the area into blocks and displace outcrops.

In places, limestones alongside these faults have been mineralized to form the iron ore deposits so important in local industrial development. **Hematite**-bearing solutions descended into the limestones filling open faults and solution cavities as well as replacing the limestone itself.

EXCURSION DETAILS
Part 1

Cars should be parked near the crossroads at the northwest corner of Birkrigg Common (280746). The map (Figure 4.1) shows access roads, Locations 1 to 5 and the Formations described.

Location 1 (281745) is the old quarry area near the crossroads. Examine the main features of the pale grey Park Limestone, much sought after for lime burning and iron smelting, due to its low mud content. Its bedding is poorly developed, so fault displacements are difficult to determine, though a **slickensided** surface can be seen on the north face of the quarry. Its closely spaced irregular **joints** allow it to disintegrate into scree. **Stylolites** (teeth and socket structures) can be found. There are some fossils: crinoid ossicles (which look like Polo mints), broken brachiopod shells and corals.

Location 2 (283740) is the old quarry area south of the Common. This, only 2–3 m deep, is alongside the highest point on the road south of the Common.

Approach from Location 1 along a grassy track or by road. An irregular bedding plane separates the Park Limestone from the overlying Urswick Limestone. The rocks are the same colour, but the Urswick Limestone is very well bedded and lacks the closely spaced joints of the Park Limestone. Here the boundary could be conformable as there is no sign of erosion. Elsewhere the boundary is regarded as a non-sequence (a period of non-deposition). Once identified, follow the boundary northwards; the Park Limestone forms the escarpment and the Urswick Limestone the summit plateau.

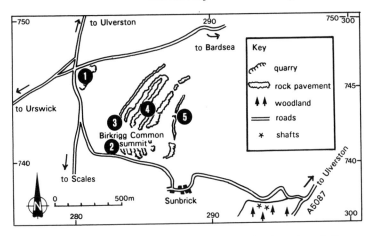

Figure 4.1 A sketch map of the Birkrigg area, showing Locations 1–5.

Location 3 (283742) is Birkrigg Common summit. On a clear day the trig point or a point 100 m to its north is an excellent vantage point to observe the effects of geology on the relief of the southern Lake District. The domed skyline of Black Combe on Skiddaw Group rocks to the northwest contrasts with the craggy outlines of the Coniston Fells on Borrowdale Volcanic Group rocks. The dissected plateau of Silurian rocks occupies the middle ground between Kirkby Moor to the northwest and Cartmel to the east. The Ellerside fault forms a prominent north–south trending escarpment along the east side of the Cartmel peninsula. Ingleborough may be visible to the east and occasionally Snowdonia to the southwest.

Location 4 (285743) is on the eastern (dip) slope of Birkrigg Common, following bedding planes of Urswick Limestone sloping at 10–15°. Solution has etched the pavement, forming **clints** and **grykes**. Well-developed bedding planes and a joint spacing of 1–3 m allow such surfaces to develop on the Urswick Limestone. Clean surfaces show pseudobrecciation (dark blotches which form irregular patterns in the lighter-coloured limestone), probably caused by burrowing animals disturbing newly deposited sediment. Look for characteristic Asbian stage fossils like *Lithostrotion* (see Figure 1.4c), *Dibunophyllum* (see Figure 1.4d) and the long-ranging *Palaeosmilia murchisoni* (see Figure 1.4e). Patches of lichen may make the fossils and pseudobrecciation difficult to find.

37

Location 5 (287742) is a depression east of Birkrigg Common. Walk down-dip to Appleby Slack, a long depression running north to south across the Common. This is probably underlain by the Woodbine Shale, a persistent, impermeable 4 m thick band, bringing groundwater to the surface at the spring originally supplying the farm at Sunbrick. The eastern side of the depression is a steep scarp, the west a gentle dip slope. This pattern is repeated on a miniature scale along the east of the Common.

Part 2

Take the road from Ulverston, signposted South Ulverston, past the Glaxo factory. Park by the Bay Horse Inn (313776), Canal Foot, near Ulverston. There are public toilets nearby. The map (Figure 4.2) shows Locations 6 to 10 and the main geological features.

Location 6 (312781) is Plumpton Bight. Walk 300 m northwards along the coast from the Bay Horse Inn to low cliffs and a wave-cut platform. The Park Limestone here shows the same 10–15° east-southeast dip as at Birkrigg Common. As soon as you reach the low cliff, a minor **dip-fault** is indicated by a 1 m band of **brecciated** limestone, cemented by calcite and **hematite**. Water seeps out of an irregular bedding plane at the foot of the cliff. Large coral colonies up to 1 m in diameter occur on the wave-cut platform, beginning 20 m past the fault. Species are few, *Lithostrotion martini* and *Lithostrotion minus* the most common. Gastropods and crinoids are also present.

Location 7 (312784) is at the eastern end of a small wood beside the coastal track. Piles of waste rock, hematized limestone and red soil mark the eastern end of the hematite vein best seen at Location 9.

The west-northwest fault which runs close to Plumpton Hall throws Carboniferous limestones against the Silurian Bannisdale Formation (formerly Bannisdale Slate). These Silurian slates are best exposed at Tridley Point (318786). Elsewhere the Carboniferous–Silurian junction is unconformable, with the two lowest Carboniferous units, the Basement Beds and the Martin Limestone, being either thin or absent. The older Carboniferous beds are visible as you walk inland.

Walk north along the path, turning inland along the lane passing Plumpton Hall. Turn left along an unfenced road through the fields, just before the bridge over the railway.

Location 8 (310786) is in the woodland west of Plumpton Hall. Enter the wood to the left of the road. The open cavity of a working in a small

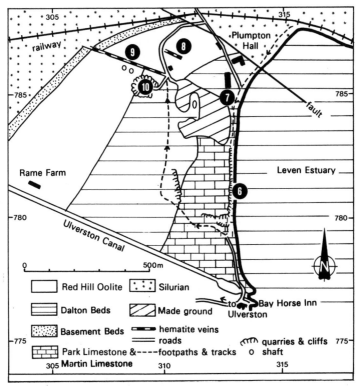

Figure 4.2 A geological sketch map of the Plumpton area, showing Locations 6–10. (Adapted from Rose and Dunham (1977) Geology and Hematite Deposits of South Cumbria, *Econ. Mem. Geol. Survey*, Sheet 58.)

hematite vein in the Red Hill **Oolite** is visible. This vein is parallel to the much larger one at the next location.

Location 9 (308786) is Iron Pit, Spring Wood. Where the road bends round to the left, cross the field to the wood on the opposite (west) side of the road. Along the northern edge of the wood is one of the few local indications of a hematite vein at the surface. This vein, first worked in 1220, follows a west-northwest trending fault, and is now a deep, water-filled open cut. *Take great care. Keep away from steep slopes.* At the extreme western end, both walls are in Red Hill Oolite, the hanging wall (the downthrown, southern side) being partly replaced by

39

hematite. To the east the hanging wall is in the Dalton Beds, not easily replaced by hematite, so the vein became less productive. The cut walls are clearly hematized and the brown porous rock of the waste tips is dolomitized limestone. *Avoid the disused shafts* (shown on Figure 4.2), which would have entered the mineralized area on the hanging wall side of the fault. Permission to visit this and other locations away from the road and paths should be sought from Mr G. Clark, Buckman Hall, Thwaites, Millom (Tel: 0229 716226).

Location 10 (308785) is Iron Pit, Spring Wood Quarry. The Red Hill Oolite here resembles the Park Limestone, looking more like pale calcareous sandstone than true oolite. It forms a scarp along the west side of the road. The Dalton Beds are much darker and well-bedded with shale partings. The boundary between the two Formations on the back wall of the quarry is difficult to locate, due to interbedding of light and dark limestones and superficial dark staining of the Red Hill Oolite. The side walls of the quarry are in the Dalton Beds.

The lower parts of the Dalton Beds are highly fossiliferous, the distinctive brachiopod, *Delepinia carinata* with its straight hinge line, and the solitary corals *Caninia*, *Clisiophyllum*, *Koninckophyllum* and *Palaeosmilia murchisoni* being common.

Permission to visit Iron Spring Wood Quarry should be sought from Cumbria Contracting, Crooklands (Tel: 05395 67488).

Return towards the car park at Canal Foot by going southward through the fields. The footpath is parallel to woods on the left. There is a 20 m high quarry face in the upper part of the Dalton Beds, 70 m east of the path in the second field. The path bends round to the left in the third field. A stile beside a gate leads to a concrete roadway between houses and gardens. This takes you back to the shore, about 250 m north of Canal Foot.

5 · The Windermere Group south of Torver

David Kelly *Excursion Secretary, Cumberland Geological Society*

PURPOSE

To investigate a sequence of Upper Silurian rocks south of Torver; and to appreciate how glacial erosion of the different rocks (including a minor igneous intrusion) has affected the scenery.

PRACTICAL DETAILS

This is quite a long half-day excursion with about 6 km to walk. Private transport is essential to reach the starting point, 1.5 km southwest of Torver on the A593, where there is parking space for several cars. Torver has two pubs and there is a wider range of services in Coniston and Broughton-in-Furness. There are no restrictions on access, as the route follows public footpaths and crosses National Park access land. Appropriate clothing and strong, suitable footwear are recommended, as the route is quite hilly and very wet in places.

OS MAPS: 1:50 000 Sheet 96 or 97
          1:25 000 Outdoor Leisure Map, The English Lakes, South Western area

GEOLOGICAL SETTING

The rocks of the area are deep-sea sediments, largely deposited by **turbidity** currents during the later part of the Silurian Period. The rocks we see from Location 3 onwards belong to the Coniston Subgroup (formerly the Coniston Grit, see Tables 1 and 5.1), but there are no published, up-to-date geological maps of the area. Evidence of bottom-dwelling organisms is unusual in this type of deposit. Fossil graptolites have been recorded, but are very difficult to find.

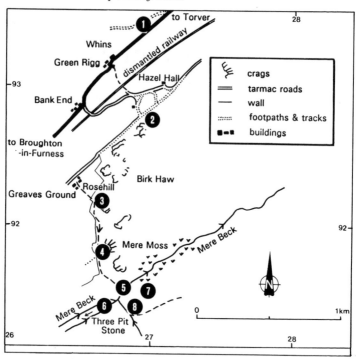

Figure 5.1 The excursion route from Whins on the A593 to Mere Beck.

At the end of the Silurian Period the area was affected by the **Caledonian orogeny**. Compression from the northwest and southeast caused folding, which resulted in the rocks here dipping steeply southeast. We follow their sequence, working from north to south down-dip to the younger rocks. The area has been affected by minor intrusions, trending northeast–southwest, probably also of Caledonian age.

Glacial troughs border the area. The Coniston Valley runs north to south and the Torver Valley branches from it, running northeast–southwest parallel to the strike. The Torver Valley is higher than the Coniston Valley and must have formed at a stage when the Coniston glacier divided, allowing some ice into the Torver Valley.

The relief is a series of ridges and troughs running parallel to the strike, the ridges consisting of the harder, coarser rocks, and the troughs following the finer-grained rocks more susceptible to glacial erosion.

EXCURSION DETAILS

Location 1 (270933) is the rather striking old quarry face above the layby at Whins. This is 1.5 km southwest of Torver on the northwest side of the A593, 150 m southwest of a junction with a minor road. Park here and walk to Locations 2–8.

The rocks in the quarry are steeply dipping turbidite siltstones and fine sandstones interbedded with mudstones showing a vertical **cleavage**. In the southwest part of the quarry, quartz-filled **tension gashes** are seen in a 1 m band which dips at about 20° across the rock face.

Walk 300 m southwest along the A593 to the houses at Green Rigg. Notice the small **drumlin** and **roches moutonnées** on the valley floor below to the left. Take the public footpath which descends steeply across a field to the dismantled Foxfield to Coniston railway. Walk up the rough road on the opposite side of the valley. Pass through a metal gate and after 50 m take the track which turns sharply to the right. When you reach a narrow tarmac road cross into the small disused quarry opposite.

Location 2 (270927) is this old quarry beside the road 200 m southwest of Hazel Hall. The rocks here and in the valley floor are dark mudstones with paler siltstone and sandstone bands. These are probably the Stennerly Mudstone of the Wray Castle Formation (formerly the Upper Coldwell Beds). The valley is cut into the softer rocks, though it may also follow the line of a major fault. Graptolites have been recorded from the quarry but are very rare.

OLD NAMES		NEW NAMES	
Coniston Grit Group	Yewbank Sandstone Formation	Yewbank Formation	Coniston Subgroup
		Moorhouse Formation	
		Poolscar Formation	
	Salthouse Mudstone Formation	Latrigg Formation	
	Poolscar Sandstone Formation	Gawthwaite Formation	
Coldwell Group	Stennerly Mudstone Formation	Wray Castle Formation	Tranearth Subgroup

Table 5.1 The Windermere Group succession south of Torver showing both old and new lithostratigraphic names.

43

Walk 300 m along the road to a gate and continue for another 200 m to Rosehill. Take the gravel path (between the buildings) which soon becomes a cart track. Carry on through two gates to Location 3, 50 m past the second gate.

Location 3 (266922) is the area of exposures southeast of this track. The higher relief with small crags corresponds to an overlying sandstone unit, probably the Gawthwaite (formerly the Poolscar Sandstone) Formation. Beds up to 2 m thick show grey–green **greywacke** sandstones weathering rusty brown. Fresh specimens show grains up to 3 mm in diameter with clearly visible mica and green volcanic material.

Continue along the track for 400 m to a pond on the left. Walk 50 m up the bracken-covered slope to the foot of the crags.

Location 4 (267919) is this craggy area east of the track. Coarse greywacke sandstones with occasional **flute casts** at their base fine upwards to siltstones showing **laminations**, **cross-laminations** and slump structures. Mudstones occur at the top of each sequence where finer beds show a vertical cleavage.

Return to the track and follow it as far as a white gate in a wall. Turn left just before this gate along a path which climbs to a col and then descends to the marshy depression of Mere Moss.

Location 5 (268916) is the valley of Mere Beck around Mere Moss. This is underlain by the Latrigg (formerly the Salthouse Mudstone) Formation. This slightly silty, unlaminated rock is exposed on small knolls to the left (northwest) of the path before you reach the valley. Mere Beck drains to the northeast but this part of the valley was probably eroded by ice or subglacial water which flowed southwest. Mere Moss is one of many old lake beds in the area. Walk 100–200 m to the southwest from Location 5 to a minor ridge.

Location 6 (266914) is this minor ridge immediately southwest of Mere Moss. A 5–10 m wide, pink microgranite **sill**, which is appreciably harder than the surrounding mudstone, forms the ridge. Feldspar **phenocrysts** about 1–2 mm in diameter occur in a fine to medium groundmass with visible quartz and **biotite**.

Look along Mere Moss to the northeast towards Location 7 where the sill again forms a minor ridge. This seems to be out of line with Location 6, either because the sill is transgressive (cutting across the bedding) or because it is displaced by a fault trending northwest–

southeast through the small valleys at the sides of the depression. Walk across the marshy ground to Location 7.

Location 7 (269915) is this minor ridge in Mere Moss with a very good exposure of the microgranite, where the igneous rock and its strongest **joint** set run parallel to the bedding of the country rock, thus proving it to be a sill. Leave Mere Moss by climbing a minor valley to the southeast beside a yew tree.

Location 8 (269914) is the high ground southeast of Mere Beck. Examine the rocks at the top of the ridge. These are greywackes of the upper part of the Coniston Subgroup, rather finer-grained than similar rocks lower down in the Subgroup. Several weathered exposures in the many rocky knolls show iron staining with red nodules.

This is a good vantage point. The surrounding subdued landscape of Windermere Group rocks is clearly different from the higher, craggy relief of Dow Crag, Coniston Old Man and Wetherlam on Borrowdale Volcanic Group rocks to the north.

Retrace your steps to Location 1.

6 · The Eskdale Granite

Brian Young *British Geological Survey, Edinburgh*

PURPOSE

To examine the Eskdale Granite, its contacts with Borrowdale Volcanic and Skiddaw Group rocks; and to look at examples of late stage alteration of the granite and of **hematite** mineralization.

PRACTICAL DETAILS

The excursion is in two parts, each lasting about half a day and each returning to its starting point.

Part 1 starts at Dalegarth Station (174007), where there is ample parking for cars and a small coach. Part 2 starts from the Eskdale Green to Ulpha road at the junction with the Devoke Water track (171977). A small number of cars and a minibus can be parked there. Walking distances and times should be judged by studying the routes given and the appropriate map (Figures 6.2 and 6.3 respectively). Appropriate windproof clothing and suitable strong footwear are necessary.

OS MAPS: 1:25 000 Outdoor Leisure Map, The English Lakes, South Western area

1:50 000 Sheets 89 and 96

BGS MAP: 1:25 000 Sheet SD 19 Devoke Water and Ulpha

GEOLOGICAL SETTING

The Eskdale Intrusion is the largest exposure of the granitic **batholith** underlying the central Lake District. There is a well-exposed northern outcrop consisting mainly of granite and microgranite and a poorly exposed southern outcrop consisting largely of **granodiorite**. Age relations are not clear but limited field evidence suggests the granodiorite is the older. Rubidium/Strontium ages of 429 +/− 4 **Ma** for the granite and 428 +/− 22 Ma for the granodiorite have been recorded. Figure 6.1 is a general geological map of the outcrop and the areas visited on the excursion.

These plutonic rocks are almost entirely emplaced (intruded) within Borrowdale Volcanic Group rocks. They are also in contact with Skiddaw Group rocks in the core of a northeast–southwest trending anticline near Devoke Water and Ravenglass. The Borrowdale Volcanic Group country rocks dip gently north on the northern flank of the granite but more steeply south on its southern flank. The original roof of the granite was probably relatively flat and not much higher than present exposures.

The granite is coarse-grained and pale pink, composed of pink **perthitic feldspar**, quartz and a little **plagioclase**. Pale **muscovite** is usually present and sometimes a little brown **biotite**. Finer-grained microgranites are common, resembling the coarser-grained granite in composition, but with very variable textures. Much is **porphyritic**, commonly with both large quartz and feldspar **phenocrysts** set in a finer groundmass, though rocks with only one type of phenocryst are often found. Non-porphyritic (aphyric) varieties, with crystals of more uniform sizes, are also common. Some microgranites occur near the contact where they may be chilled marginal phases. More extensive and highly irregular masses of microgranite within the granite are frequent too.

The granites and microgranites have been much altered. Micas are often partly replaced by reddish-brown hematite and feldspars often partly altered to scaly **sericite**. Locally dark, almost black, **tourmaline** replaces feldspars with sprays of crystals on joint faces. Near contacts, granites and microgranites are altered in places to a variety of **greisens**. Consisting mainly of quartz and mica with locally abundant **topaz**, their presence is due to the alteration of crystallized granite by hot fluids in the final stages of cooling. Faulting has occurred at several periods since the granite was intruded. Some faults acted as channels for mineralizing fluids, especially those carrying hematite, during a major period of iron mineralization probably in Cretaceous or Tertiary times.

EXCURSION DETAILS

Part 1

The granite, its contacts on Bleatarn Hill, and the iron ore deposits at Boot are the subjects of this part of the excursion. See Figure 6.2 for details of the geology and locations visited.

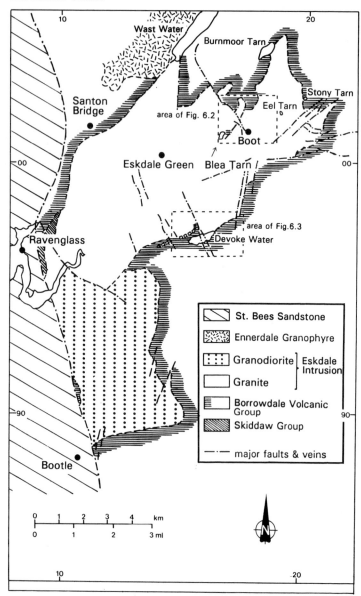

Figure 6.1 A geological sketch map of the Eskdale Intrusion.

Park in Dalegarth Station car park. Walk east from the station to Brook House Hotel and turn left into Boot village. The flat ground is on the alluvial deposits of the River Esk and its tributary, the Whillan Beck. Notice the thick dry-stone walls with rounded boulders (usually of Eskdale Granite) cleared from the fields. Cross the Mill Bridge in Boot village, and follow the track north and diagonally uphill. There are many ice-smoothed outcrops (**roches moutonnées**) on the hillside. At first these are mainly coarse-grained granites, with microgranites further up the slope.

Location 1 (177018), a group of ruined buildings, provides a good viewpoint. The prominent hills to the east across Whillan Beck are Little Barrow and Great Barrow. The top of Great Barrow is an **outlier** of **hornfelsed** (fine-grained, hardened) Borrowdale Volcanic Group **tuffs**, part of the roof of the Eskdale Granite. Bear north-northeast across the open moorland to a stile almost at the eastern end of the outermost stone wall or intake fence. Go into the field and follow the wall downhill to about 100 m above the gate.

Location 2 (180024) is a microgranite outcrop with many quartz phenocrysts. At its western edge the microgranite becomes finer-grained with **aplitic** (sugary) textures near its contact with Borrowdale Volcanic Group tuffs. At this well-exposed contact the intensely hornfelsed Borrowdale Volcanic Group rocks are **brecciated** and veined by pale pink microgranite. There is a small exposure of a quartz–mica greisen about 10 m east of the contact. This is a distinctive, sparkling white rock, composed almost entirely of quartz and mica with a few grains of white topaz. It is identical in texture with the surrounding microgranite. Greisens are common near the margins of the Eskdale Granite, where volatiles were trapped against the relatively impermeable hornfelsed contact rocks. Return southwest-ward from the granite contact across the breast of the hill, passing Location 1.

Location 3 (172016) is a fenced shaft at the southern end of Brown Band. A broad hollow just west of Brown Band marks the north-northwest–south-southeast trending course of a major fault running between Wastwater Screes and Boot. Its southern part carries the hematite worked last century at Nab Gill mine above Boot. Continue southwestwards to the southern part of Bleatarn Hill, which is mainly microgranite, varying from markedly porphyritic, with quartz or feldspar phenocrysts or both, to aphyric in texture.

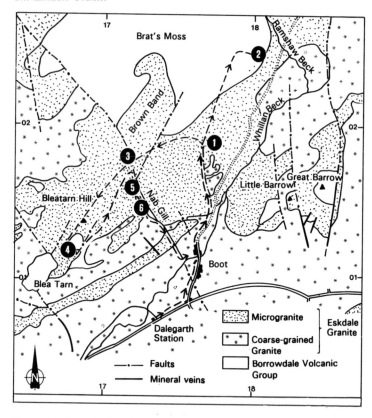

Figure 6.2 A geological sketch map of the Boot area, showing Locations 1–6.

Location 4 (168011) is a small outlier of hornfelsed tuff, cropping out on the southwestern shoulder of Bleatarn Hill 20 m beyond the summit towards Blea Tarn. This contact is even and unbrecciated. Bleatarn Hill is an excellent viewpoint. To the south of Boot is Gate Crag (185997), a prominent wall-like feature consisting of Borrowdale Volcanic Group lavas and tuffs just above the granite, the roof of which can be traced below the crag. This feature ends abruptly at Hartley Crag (181995) where a major fault displaces the granite contact 1 km to the south. The undulating fell country west of Hartley Crag is mainly granite. Birkby Fell (145960) and Yoadcastle (157952) in the far distance, to the south and southwest beyond Devoke Water, are volcanic rocks above the granite.

Note the fault-guided northeast–southwest trending gully on the southwest side of Bleatarn Hill. Contacts between microgranites and tuffs are very clear, as is their displacement by faulting. Return to Location 3, and follow the hollow southeastwards.

Location 5 (172015) is the old opencast workings where the Nab Gill vein and its western branch were worked at the head of the gill. Small exposures of brecciated hematite can be seen in its southern corner. Open **stopes** on the high ground, west of the hollow, show excellent, small, unworked sections of the vein with '**kidney-ore**' forming bands roughly parallel to the vein walls. *These open workings are dangerous. Do not approach too close and under no circumstances enter the fenced-off area. Do not attempt to enter any of the mines.*

The steep-sided gully of Nab Gill follows the Nab Gill vein. Although originally a stream valley, the gully has been deepened by opencast mining and the collapse of underground workings. Nab Gill mine was worked, mainly last century, from five **adits** in addition to the opencasts. Much of the vein filling is brecciated, hematite-stained granite with two large ore shoots of good quality hematite, mainly 'kidney ore', often broken into the characteristic 'pencils'. There is also a little crystalline **specularite** and some manganese oxides. **Gangue** minerals such as quartz, **dolomite** and calcite are scarce.

Location 6 (174013) is the collapsed entrance to No. 2 Level. Note the series of branch veins alongside with excellent bands of 'kidney ore'. *Please do not hammer this outcrop.* You can collect good samples from the old spoil heaps especially towards the fell top.

The Eskdale hematite deposits are thought to be part of the widespread iron mineralization which produced the enormous replacement deposits in the Carboniferous limestones of West and South Cumbria. The origin and ages of these are a matter for conjecture.

Ore was taken down the fell on a self-acting inclined tramway whose bed we follow downhill to the old mine buildings and loading bay at the abandoned terminus of the original 'La'al Ratty', the Ravenglass to Eskdale railway. Walk east back to Mill Bridge and to your vehicle.

Part 2

The granites, greisen and late stage mineralization are the subjects of Part 2. Figure 6.3 shows details of the geology and the locations visited.

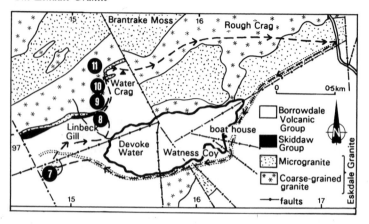

Figure 6.3 A geological sketch map of the Devoke Water area, showing Locations 7–11.

Start from the junction of the rough track to Devoke Water (no unauthorized vehicles, please!) with the unclassified Eskdale Green to Ulpha road (171977). There is parking space for several cars. Follow the track to the eastern end of Devoke Water, more or less along the unexposed faulted southern boundary of the Eskdale Granite. Till mantles the ground with occasional knolls, mainly of microgranite, north of the track. Fine-grained andesites and tuffs crop out to the south on Seat How beyond the peat-filled hollow of Tewit Moss.

Follow the southern shore of Devoke Water. Much of the route is drift-covered with brecciated andesites and tuffs exposed above. Rather shattered granites and microgranites crop out between two roughly north–south trending faults on the rising ground (159967) south of the path near Watness Coy. Devoke Water appears to be a rock basin lake dammed in part by a low ridge of till at its western end. Cross the boulder-clay-covered ground from the western end of the lake to a low rocky knoll south of the indistinct track.

Location 7 (148967), this knoll, is an inlier of pale, porphyritic, ice-smoothed microgranite within Borrowdale Volcanic Group rocks. The microgranite has many quartz and feldspar phenocrysts. Much of it is altered to a pale quartz–mica greisen, adjacent to several quartz veins. Despite intense alteration, much of the original texture, including residual quartz phenocrysts, remains. Vertical bands of coarse-grained specular hematite cut the greisen northwest of the knoll summit.

The northern part of the Eskdale Granodiorite to the west and southwest forms featureless moorland. Return to the western end of Devoke Water, turning north to cross Linbeck Gill near its exit from the lake. Negotiate the boggy ground south of Water Crag, where you will find Locations 8 to 11.

Location 8 (152972) is the lowest outcrop on the southwestern slope, where exposures of pale fawn hornfelsed silty mudstones of the Skiddaw Group show conspicuous slabby weathering along **cleavage** planes.

Location 9 (152973) is a prominent, ice-smoothed, coarse-grained granite exposure further up the hillside where much of the granite has been altered to greisen. The main greisen type on Water Crag is a quartz–topaz rock. Although easily mistaken for pale granite, close examination shows that it consists of grey quartz and pale cream topaz with poorly developed crystals up to 8 mm across and a lustrous basal cleavage. There are traces of deep purple fluorite (CaF_2) on some joint surfaces, and locally small concentrations of grey, metallic minerals which include native bismuth (Bi), bismuthinite (Bi_2S_3), **molybdenite** (MoS_2) and arsenopyrite (FeAsS). A few rounded aggregates of pink **andalusite** up to 3 mm across can be seen in the easternmost exposure of the greisen. Follow the eastern edge of the greisen outcrop uphill.

Location 10 (153973) is the western edge of the hilltop, where coarse-grained pink granite forms ice-smoothed exposures. Near the granite–volcanic rock contact quartz–topaz greisen crops out again. Small exposures of slabby Skiddaw Group hornfels occur a few metres to the east, with small crags of hornfelsed andesites further east again, but their contacts are not exposed. A 1 m wide rib of a striking pink and white quartz–andalusite rock crops out adjacent to the inferred contact with the granite. *Please do not hammer any of these exposures.*

Location 11 (153976) is reached by following the granite contact around the northern and western flanks of Water Crag, where hornfelsed andesites are in very clear contact with unaltered granite.

Return to the Ulpha road, either by retracing the route along the southern shores of Devoke Water, or by continuing north-northeast along the ridge to Rough Crag (162977), then walking due east across the open moorland to your vehicle.

This contribution is published with the approval of the Director of the British Geological Survey (NERC).

7 · Volcanic Rocks of northern Wasdale

Mike Petterson *British Geological Survey*

PURPOSE

To examine rocks of the Lower Borrowdale Volcanic Group; and to distinguish lavas from rocks formed by explosive eruptions (**air fall tuffs** and **ignimbrites**) and epiclastic deposits (reworked and re-deposited volcanic debris).

PRACTICAL DETAILS

One very full day or two comfortable days' excursions, west and east respectively of Scoat Tarn, involving some 15 km of rough walking and a total ascent of 1000 m. Appropriate windproof clothing and suitable strong footwear are essential. *This is a physically demanding excursion and is not recommended in bad weather.* Parking is limited, for cars and minibuses only, just east of Overbeck Bridge (168069), and occasionally for up to four cars by Netherbeck Bridge (162066). The nearest pubs and public toilets are at Wasdale Head and at Nether Wasdale, with cafés and shops in Gosforth. The map (Figure 7.1) shows the locations visited, the routes and the main features of the geology.

OS MAPS: 1:50 000 Sheet 89
          1:25 000 Outdoor Leisure maps of the Lake District, North Western and South Western areas

GEOLOGICAL SETTING

This excursion traverses spectacular mountain scenery, including the peaks of Haycock (797 m) and Red Pike (821 m). The strenuous walking required is rewarded by superb views of the Central Fells,

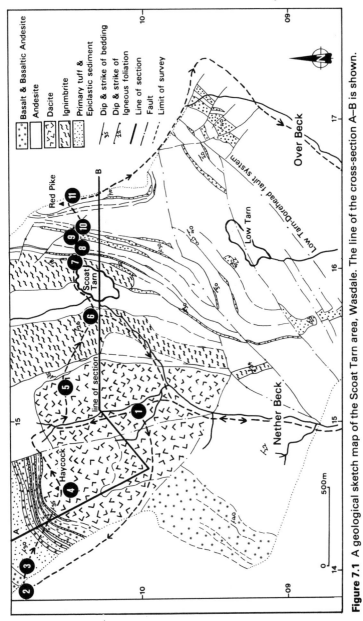

Figure 7.1 A geological sketch map of the Scoat Tarn area, Wasdale. The line of the cross-section A–B is shown.

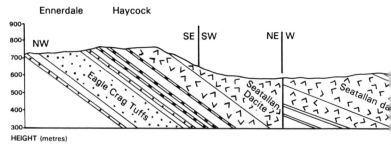

Ennerdale, Wasdale and Eskdale, and on clear days, Galloway and the Isle of Man.

There are two distinct divisions of the (Ordovician) Borrowdale Volcanic Group (BVG) rocks: (1) The Lower BVG, dominated by **andesitic** and **basaltic** lavas, **sills** and interbedded volcaniclastic deposits (a mixture of primary air fall tuffs, reworked volcanic sandstones and siltstones); (2) The Upper BVG, dominated by thick ignimbrite sheets and epiclastic sequences, with some andesite and basalt. This excursion studies a substantial thickness of the Lower BVG. It shows the tremendous variety in detail of volcanic deposits within the large-scale sequence of predominantly andesitic sheets in the Lower BVG.

During the Upper BVG volcanic activity became increasingly explosive with more viscous (stickier) and cooler magma than during the Lower BVG. Eruptions of the BVG took place partly on land and partly in shallow lakes. Many of the lava flows were viscous, flowing only 1–15 km after eruption. They are therefore relatively localized. An alternative idea is that many of these 'lava flows' should be regarded as peperitic sills. These intruded wet and relatively soft sediments very close to the earth's surface, with resulting interaction between the magma and water.

The geological section (Figure 7.2) illustrates the sequence and is particularly useful in following the rock succession during the excursion.

EXCURSION DETAILS

Start the excursion from Netherbeck Bridge. Head north along the footpath on the west side of Nether Beck as far as Little Lad Crag (151101), beyond which two routes are suggested. The first is more convenient but it is also more difficult as there are no paths. *It is not*

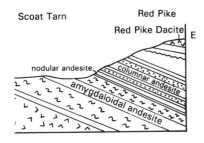

Scoat Tarn   Red Pike
Red Pike Dacite E
nodular andesite
columnar andesite
amygdaloidal andesite

Figure 7.2 A geological cross-section from Ennerdale and Haycock to Red Pike (Wasdale). The line of section is indicated on Figure 7.1, and the key is as for Figure 7.1.

recommended in bad weather. Contour westwards and then northwest-wards around Brown Band to the watershed between Ennerdale and Wasdale (138110). You will find it easier to walk up the normal path to the col between Haycock and Great Scoat Fell, before turning west to Locations 1–4. In either case, climb Haycock and proceed to the western shore of Scoat Tarn before climbing Red Pike. The recommended return route is over Dore Head (175096) into the Overbeck valley. The alternative, for experienced parties only, is to descend Red Pike to Scoat Tarn and return down the Nether Beck valley.

Location 1 (151101) is Little Lad Crag. The Seatallan **Dacite** is exposed here, light grey to pink in colour and very clearly **flow-banded**. Its strongly developed **jointing** gives the dacite a granite-like appearance. Fresh surfaces show that it consists of 3–6 mm **feldspar phenocrysts** set in a light-coloured, very fine-grained matrix, a devitrified glass, giving a characteristic rough, jagged, fracture surface.

Location 2 (138109) is just south of the boundary fence between Ennerdale and Wasdale. Walk east and then southeast close to the boundary, as the best outcrops of individual units may be either side of it. The first outcrops are a series of rubbly, basaltic lavas with interbedded volcanic sandstones. The lavas are dark-coloured and quite thin (20–40 m). Like many of the lavas and sills in this sequence they have two distinct **facies**: (1) massive to flow-banded/flow-folded centres; (2) highly **brecciated** margins. The centre of the lava remained hot and liquid whilst the outer, cooler margins solidified and were autobrecciated (broken up) as the lava flowed downhill. The alternative explanation is that the brecciation may be a feature of a high level peperitic sill. Notice the generally **porphyritic** texture of the basaltic lavas. **Pyroxene** (generally dark in colour, now

chloritized) and lighter-coloured feldspar phenocrysts are set in a fine, dark to medium-grey groundmass. These sheets exhibit slaggy, rubbly, cindery margins typical of one type of basalt lava flow.

Location 3 (140108) is 200 m further east along the wall, between Little Gowder Crag and Haycock summit. Here the Eagle Crag **Tuffs** (**lithified** primary and reworked volcanic ash and **lapilli**) overlie the basaltic lavas. At 150–200 m the tuffs are by far the thickest volcaniclastic sequence of the BVG in the Western Lakes, weathering along bedding planes to form flaggy blocks rather than the more massive outcrops of the lavas. Particle sizes vary greatly. Sedimentary structures include parallel and **cross laminations** (layers less than 1 cm thick), **rip-up clasts**, dewatering features and erosional surfaces. The clasts are andesitic, originating from **pyroclastic** air fall eruptions and reworked/re-deposited volcanic detritus. Between the top of the Eagle Crag Tuffs and Location 4, another sequence of thin basaltic andesite sheets and interbedded sediments crops out.

Location 4 (145107) is the summit of Haycock. Unlike the underlying basaltic andesite the rock here is a light-coloured, strongly flow-jointed porphyritic dacite, best seen along the northern rim of the summit plateau. This underlies the very distinctive 200–300 m thick dacite sheet that extends over 7–10 km, the Seatallan Dacite, seen at Little Lad Crag. Descend from Haycock to the col between it and Great Scoat Fell. Follow the path that turns right (south) and go steeply downhill for about 300 m to a flatter area. Cross a stream valley, leaving the path to cross boggy ground in a generally southeasterly direction. Contour to maintain height and examine outcrops en route. An easier but longer way is to continue down the path to join Nether Beck (which you follow northeast to Scoat Tarn) just below Little Lad Crag.

Location 5 (153105) is where thinly bedded epiclastic sediments overlie brecciated Seatallan Dacite. A succession of beds trending at 330° form the southern slopes of Great Scoat Fell, indicating the local strike of the Lower BVG.

Location 6 (157105) is a distinctive round-topped crag just west of Scoat Tarn and 100 m north of Nether Beck. The 'trap' scenery in front, on the western slopes of Red Pike, is impressive. Prominent benches mark the tops of the resistant andesites and ignimbrites. The flat benches are due to more rapid erosion of less resistant interbedded volcanic sediments.

Figure 7.3 Panoramic photograph of the crags below Red Pike, viewed from west of Scoat Tarn. The accompanying field sketch highlights the volcanic trap scenery. *Photo*: M. Petterson

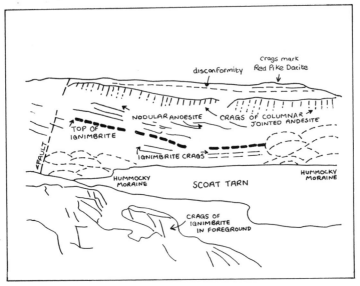

Figure 7.3 highlights the main features of the view looking east towards Red Pike. Ignimbrites crop out either side of Scoat Tarn here and at Location 7. They form during highly explosive **pyroclastic flow** eruptions. The materials are **vesiculated** pumice, **lithic** fragments (andesite to dacite here), glass shards and ash. The particles were fluidized, had a low viscosity and flowed considerable distances very quickly. When they came to rest the weight of the deposit compressed the particles, which welded together to form the ignimbrite. Pumices flattened, forming lenticular **fiamme**, giving ignimbrites their characteristic streaky appearance, the **eutaxitic** texture. Lithic fragments were usually stronger, didn't flatten, and stand proud on the outcrop.

If you are tired or time presses, return down the Nether Beck valley. The exposures that follow are far too interesting to miss. So, come back another day!

Location 7 (161 105) is by the northeast corner of Scoat Tarn. Lithic

Figure 7.4 Bedded volcaniclastic rocks at Location 10. Notice the alternating coarse lapilli and fine silt-sized layers and their contrasting bedding styles. *Photo*: M. Petterson

fragments, mainly **rhyodacitic**, stand proud of the rock face, and vary from fine ash to lapilli, larger than a peanut in size. The ignimbrite matrix is mainly tuff, often the main bulk of explosive pyroclastic flow eruptions. Locations 8–10 are on the steep slopes between Scoat Tarn and the summit ridge of Red Pike. Figure 7.2 gives their rock sequence.

Location 8 (162105) is the outcrop of a highly **amygdaloidal** andesite, forming a lower craggy outcrop and containing spherical nodules of **epidote** (generally pale green in colour) which fill former vesicles. Immediately above the andesite are bedded volcanic sandstones and a very thin cindery, brecciated andesite.

Location 9 (163106) is where overlying columnar andesite forms impressive crags following the strike. This rock has feldspar phenocrysts set in a fine-grained grey groundmass.

Location 10 (164105) is where a noticeable sequence of bedded volcaniclastic sediments, 10–11 m. thick, overlies the columnar andesite, cropping out over 1 km to form a very prominent bench. Bedding and grain size vary considerably in these sediments. Figure 7.4 shows how clast sizes range in these beds up to 4 cm in diameter, locally grading into breccias with andesitic blocks of up to 10 cm. From Location 10, head up to the Red Pike ridge. Several andesite and dacite sheets crop out en route. Note the slight angular **disconformity** between the volcanic rocks exposed at the summit of Red Pike and those lower down (see Figure 7.3). This break in sequence was probably caused by contemporaneous volcanically induced faulting.

Location 11 (166106) is just south of the summit of Red Pike where the light-coloured, strongly porphyritic and flow-banded Red Pike andesite is exposed. This caps the local volcanic sequence. Look at the view! Haycock, Seatallan and Middle Fell lie to the west; Pillar, Steeple and Ennerdale to the north; the Central Fells to the east-southeast; and Yewbarrow, the Screes and Eskdale to the south. From Red Pike, continue along the ridge to Dore Head, turning southwest to follow a path down the Overbeck valley to your vehicle. The more experienced may fancy the difficult descent to Scoat Tarn and Nether Beck.

This contribution is published with the approval of the Director of the British Geological Survey (NERC).

8 · The Permo-Trias of St Bees Headland

Tom Shipp *Past President and former General Secretary, Cumberland Geological Society*

PURPOSE

To examine the New Red Sandstone formations and their basal **unconformity**; to explore the variety of rocks in glacial deposits and beach materials; and to look at evidence of changes in sea level.

PRACTICAL DETAILS

A one-day excursion which can be split into three half days. Route A involves a 9 km walk, mainly along footpaths, returning from St Bees to Whitehaven by private or public transport (bus or train).

Routes B1 (Locations 1–3), B2 (Locations 4–5) and B3 (Locations 6–9) are half-day excursions. All routes involve some scrambling over rough ground, so suitable strong footwear and appropriate clothing should be worn. *Near cliff faces at Locations 1, 3, 4, 5, 7 and 8 safety helmets should be worn.*

Start from Kells (967165), 1.5 km south of Whitehaven, just north of the Marchon factory site. Vehicles may be parked on the roadside there and at Sandwith. St Bees beach has a large pay and display car park, public toilets and refreshment facilities. See Figure 8.1 for details of the route, locations and rock types.

OS MAPS: 1:25 000 Pathfinder 593 (Whitehaven and St Bees)
1:50 000 Sheet 89
BGS MAPS: 1:50 000 Sheet 28, Whitehaven, Solid or Drift edition

GEOLOGICAL SETTING

The St Bees Headland is an extensive but isolated plateau, rising to 142 m. It lies to the west of the broad, deeply incised, north–south trending glacial **meltwater channel** followed by the railway between Whitehaven and St Bees. The lower northern part of the upland, Kells and Woodhouse, consists of Upper Carboniferous (Westphalian) Coal Measures. The last of the many collieries, Haig Pit (967176), closed in 1986. Its workings extended several kilometres under the Solway Firth. Coal Measures shales were quarried for brick-making in the hillside behind the town cemetery (973165) until the 1970s.

The western and southern parts of the headland are the highest. They consist of the strongly jointed red St Bees Sandstone of the Triassic Sherwood Sandstone Group. This dips gently west-southwest and has been extensively quarried for building stone. It is the highest New Red Sandstone unit exposed locally, being underlain successively by St Bees Shale with its **evaporite** horizons containing **anhydrite** and **gypsum** (forms of calcium sulphate), Magnesian Limestone and Brockram. The basal **Brockram**, a **breccia**, is very thin locally, and is thought to be the edge of a series of ancient desert scree fans of Permian age which banked up against mountains where the Lake District is today. The Magnesian Limestone and evaporites probably formed in a shallow enclosed marine basin under conditions similar to parts of the present-day Persian Gulf.

Ice from the Southern Uplands of Scotland and the Lake District invaded the area during the last 2 **Ma**. Near the end of the last glaciation the Lake District ice cap melted quickly while the Irish Sea Basin was still choked with ice from Scotland. A complex series of north–south trending meltwater channels formed along the Cumbrian coastal strip as a result. Glacial **erratics** in the tills, in this case of Scottish origin (e.g. Criffel Granite), confirm that ice from Scotland was present. Pebbles from these tills are common in Fleswick Bay (945134) and along St Bees beach (around 964114). The Golf Course cliffs behind St Bees beach consist of a chaotic mixture of outwash sands, gravels and coarse blocky moraine, deposited at the end of the Devensian Glaciation, the last major ice advance.

EXCURSION DETAILS

Routes A and B1 start from Kells (967165), on the hill 1.5 km south of Whitehaven. Park on the roadside or (by previous arrangement) in one of the large car parks owned by Messrs Albright & Wilson Ltd., Marchon Division. Walk along the private road (a pedestrian right of way) which skirts the northern boundary of the Marchon factory, turning right under the bridge (966164) and walking across the field to a track. Turn south along this track to a small abandoned quarry in the hillside beyond the Marchon site.

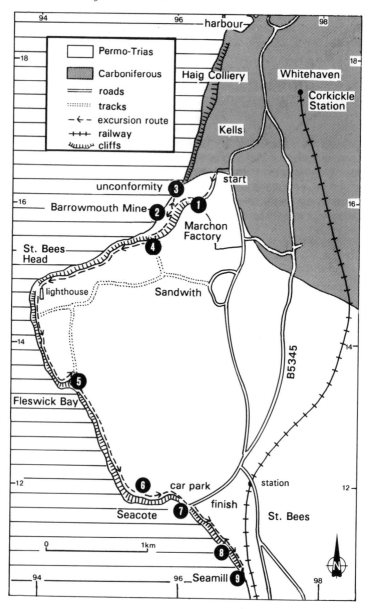

Figure 8.1 A sketch map of the St Bees Headland.

Location 1 (963160) is this quarry, now partly backfilled but still containing a few specimens of gypsum and anhydrite. These came from the Marchon drift mine, which provided anhydrite for the manufacture of sulphuric acid between the 1950s and 1970s. The quarry shows many interesting features. There is an upward gradation from shale, previously quarried for use in the anhydrite–sulphuric acid process, to sandstone. There is no clear-cut junction between the St Bees Shale and the overlying St Bees Sandstone. Fallen blocks of sandstone give clues to its origin; ripple marks, **load casts** and desiccation cracks being especially noticeable. These suggest that the sandstone was water-laid but frequently exposed to hot sun and drying winds. The normal red colour of the shales and sandstones is broken here and there by greenish layers and blotches, possibly due to the reduction of red iron(III) oxide. Soil creep has markedly increased the apparent dip of the beds at the factory end of the quarry. Measure the general dip to compare with observations elsewhere.

Walk westwards from the quarry along the track to a path running downhill parallel to the former mineral incline of the long-closed Barrowmouth **Alabaster** Mine (957157). The ruined mine buildings can be seen at the foot of the incline a few metres above sea level. The incline, presumably straight originally, is now markedly kinked. The cause of this is likely to be landslips, as there are several arcuate landslip scars and the underlying rock is shaly and lacks strength. The sandstone–shale boundary can be seen sloping southwestwards. Notice how the weathered shales produce steep vegetated slopes, whilst the well-jointed sandstone forms vertical cliffs. Walk down or alongside the incline to the ruined mine buildings.

Location 2 (957157) is by these ruins, with the springs behind showing where the **adits** were. The walls of the old buildings have been backtilted about 15° by rotational slippage. There is a small dump nearby, mainly of anhydrite. The mine, which was worked in the middle of the last century for alabaster and plaster production, failed due to the decreasing gypsum and increasing anhydrite content away from the St Bees shale outcrop. Proceed 330 m north-northeast from the mine before descending the low cliff to the foreshore. *Take care, the clay is very slippery when wet.*

Location 3 (960161) is the unconformity between the Upper Carboniferous and the Permo-Trias which is exposed in the wave-washed rock bench and low cliff above. The purplish, strongly current-bedded Coal Measure sandstone, with its eroded upper surfaces, outcrops at sea level, and is overlain by about 2 m of Brockram which penetrates open joints in places. Look at the composition of the Brockram and note how poorly sorted it is. It consists of angular fragments – mainly sandstone (probably Carboniferous), limestone (certainly Carboniferous with included corals and brachiopods), and occasional weathered lava and **tuff** pieces (probably Borrowdale Volcanic Group). The limestone **clasts** have been heavily **dolomitized**, many having hollow centres. Above the Brockram is 5 m of buff-coloured Magnesian Limestone deposited by the highly saline Zechstein Sea of Permian times. It contains a sparse fossil fauna of the bivalve *Schizodus*, and at one horizon an excellent exposure of the **trace fossil**, *Rhizocorallum*, a U-tube-shaped burrow system with web-like markings. The Magnesian Limestone passes upwards into buff-coloured and then red St Bees Shales. Return to the old mineral incline and climb back to the Cumbria Coastal Way below outcrops of St Bees Sandstone. Route B1 returns to Kells.

Route A follows the path, rising gently southwestwards. There are excellent views along the coast to the west and north and across the Solway Firth to the coast of Scotland. Notice **cross-bedding** in the St Bees Sandstone and load casts on the undersides of projecting beds. Route B2, which begins at Sandwith village (965147), joins Route A at the cottages by Birkhams Quarry.

Location 4 (956154) is this quarry (see Figure 8.2), recently reopened for the small-scale production of high-quality building stone. It shows many excellent examples of the sedimentary features previously described. Head west from the cottages along a cliff-top path winding between old cliff-edge quarries. St Bees Sandstone from these quarries has been used as a beautiful and durable building stone throughout Cumbria. It was even exported as ballast in eighteenth-century sailing ships to the American Colonies. The rock is generally sound, but *be careful*, especially in wet and windy conditions, as the path comes very close to some sheer drops. These quarries show good cross-sections of sedimentary structures.

Continue towards St Bees Lighthouse, near which a large pillar of sandstone leans away from the cliff face. Its bedding and joint planes are ideal nesting perches. *Please do not disturb either of the sites managed by the Royal Society for the Protection of Birds*. Follow the field path downhill.

Location 5 (945134) is Fleswick Bay, a steeply cut valley facing southwest, presumably incised along either a fault or a major joint plane. The beach is a thin veneer of gravel with beautifully rounded

Figure 8.2 Birkhams Quarry (Location 4). *Photo*: T. Shipp

stones of many varieties of quartz and igneous rocks. Semi-precious agate, jasper and carnelian pebbles, polished by collisions with one another and the underlying St Bees Sandstone, can also be found. These were hard clasts in the glacial drift which were then eroded and reworked by the sea.

Wave action has undercut the base of the sandstone cliffs, as well as fluting and scouring the wavecut platform exposed at low tide, and enlarging joints to help form a small cave. Springs emerge in the cave and at a prominent rock junction on the valley sides. Scramble back up the valley to the fields.

Route B1 continues 1 km northwards along a field path to the road which returns to Sandwith past Tarnflat Hall (948146). Route A turns southeastwards immediately above Fleswick Bay along the cliff path over Tomlin and South Head.

Location 6 (953119) is Pattering Holes, which seems to be a landslip area with aligned cliff-top craters marking open joints in the sandstone. There is a good view of the seaward end of the St Bees valley which is partly blocked by glacial deposits. Walk down to the promenade at St Bees. Route B3 is a circuit beginning there.

Location 7 (962117) is the southeast end of the concrete promenade, where the boulder clay cliffs begin. Near the top of the pebble beach is a huge boulder of green **vesicular andesite**, a rock of the Borrowdale Volcanic Group. This is a glacial erratic. Walk along the base of the cliffs towards Seamill (969109). Notice the astonishing variety of pebbles at the top of the beach, brought by ice from both the Lake District and Scotland. Granites, **granodiorites**, andesites, tuffs, **greywackes** and vein quartz can be found. Boulders of the local sandstones are common, the bright red Triassic contrasting with the duller brown Carboniferous.

The beach material comes mainly from the Golf Course cliffs above. Fresh landslip scars and mudflows show that erosion is still rapid. Glacial **tills** outcrop at both the top and bottom of these cliffs. In between are fluviglacial sands and gravels, contorted when ice deposited the upper, finer grained till.

Locality 8 (966112) is a peat bed in the cliff above moraine and below sand, suggesting a brief warmer period.

Locality 9 (968107), visible at low tide near an old sewage outfall just beyond the end of the cliffs at Seamill, is the exposure of tree stumps and roots in grey clay, part of a submerged forest.

Return either along a path on the cliff edge to the Seacote car park (961117) or walk along the road under the railway bridge into St Bees village which has bus stops and a railway station.

9 · The Lower Palaeozoic rocks of the Buttermere Valley

Mervyn Dodd *Past President and former Excursion Secretary, Cumberland Geological Society*

PURPOSE

To examine Skiddaw Group sediments and their structures; and to appreciate the variety of Borrowdale Volcanic Group (BVG) rocks and the effects of glaciation.

PRACTICAL DETAILS

This full-day excursion comprises three short walks from the B5289 and a steep circuit from Gatesgarth (195150), rising 500 m or so. The ground walked is open fell, boggy in places, so appropriate windproof clothing and suitable, strong footwear are essential. There are no restrictions on access. Parking space is limited, coaches not being allowed beyond Buttermere village, which has a shop, pub and public toilets. Figure 9.1 shows aspects of the geology and the locations visited.

OS MAPS: 1:25 000 Outdoor Leisure Map, The English Lakes, North Western area
1:50 000 Sheet 89
BGS MAPS: 1:25 000 Sheet, NY 12, Lorton and Loweswater

GEOLOGICAL SETTING

The Skiddaw Group rock outcrops seen on this excursion represent both the northern and southern sequences recently identified by BGS staff. The northern sequences belong to the main northwestern Lakes outcrop and are **turbidites** with mudstones (now metamorphosed to slate), and siltstones with occasional sandstones. Variations in the lithology allow the recognition of three distinct Formations in the

69

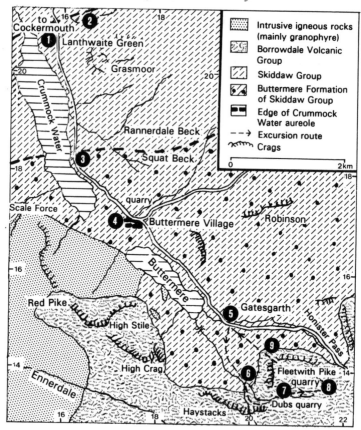

Figure 9.1 A sketch map of the Buttermere valley.

area, with the Loweswater Flags (sandstone) separating the Hope Beck Slates and the Kirk Stile Slates, respectively the oldest and youngest Skiddaw Group rocks cropping out locally. **Graded bedding** (fining upwards) and **convolute bedding** are the chief sedimentary structures. Slump folds, resembling normal folds but without **cleavages**, are common. Between deposition and the end of the **Caledonian orogeny** these rocks were folded several times, faulted and metamorphosed.

The rocks north of Hause Point (161182) illustrate the northern sequence, with the Crummock Water **aureole**, where rocks have been mildly metamorphosed by heat, extending between Hause Point and Whin Ben (166212).

The southern sequences had a similar style of deposition until a catastrophic event disrupted them with a submarine slide. This, triggered perhaps by an earthquake, transported and re-deposited much of the earlier, already compacted sediments as slumped masses (olistoliths). This sequence is the Buttermere Formation.

Lower Borrowdale Volcanic Group rocks are exposed above Buttermere between High Stile and Honister, where fine-grained, cleaved and metamorphosed **tuffs** were quarried. These tuffs and **andesitic** lavas, with amygdales (later mineral infills) and **porphyritic** textures, are the main types of volcanic rocks found there. The Ennerdale **Granophyre**, a fine-grained pink granite, crops out between Sour Milk Gill (167154) and Scale Force (151171).

Glacial landforms are best developed on the volcanic rocks. Northeast-facing slopes of Borrowdale Volcanic Group rocks contain **corries** like Bleaberry Combe (165155) with its small tarn, and Burtness Combe (175145). Fleetwith Edge, a fine stepped **arête**, and the **trough end** of Warnscale Bottom are spectacular. The west-facing slopes of Robinson on Skiddaw Group rocks are less dramatic. Buttermere and Crummock Water, originally one rock-basin lake, have been separated by the deltas of Sour Milk Gill and Sail Beck (175170). Rannerdale (162186) and Hassness (187157) have well-developed **alluvial fans**.

Slate mining ended in the 1970s but old quarries and ruined buildings remain. Abandoned copper and lead trials can be found between Gasgale Gill (163210) and west of Buttermere. Neither these nor the small iron mine once worked below Scale Force have affected the landscape much.

EXCURSION DETAILS

Location 1 (158207) is 200 m south of the cattle grid at Lanthwaite Green, with ample parking for cars or a coach. Allow up to an hour for Locations 1 and 2.

This is a fine viewpoint. Mellbreak is across Crummock Water to the southwest. Ling Comb and Bleaberry Combe, corries flanking Red Pike, are to the south. Above the road are the **truncated spurs** of Whiteside with its grey screes, and Grasmoor with the brownish screes of the Crummock Water aureole, whose gradational boundary lies between Whin Ben and Gasgale Gill. The upright Grasmoor anticline has its axis almost directly above us but is too big to recognize easily.

The best indication is the general southeast dip parallel to the road towards Buttermere.

Walk across the open ground towards Whin Ben, looking out for the mineral vein (with its small trial) snaking across the spur. Use the footbridge over Liza Beck, noticing just beyond it a thick, compact sandstone bed, part of the Loweswater Flags. Climb to the 4 m wide vein outcrop of red stained quartz. Follow the path along the contour towards Gasgale Gill.

Location 2 (166212) is on the path on the corner of the fellside overlooking Gasgale Gill. Tight recumbent folds and boudinage (sausage-shaped minor structures due to the stretching and disruption of the sandstone beds) are finely developed. These can be seen on rocks between the lower rowan tree and a holly bush on the corner of the fellside overlooking Gasgale Gill. Return to the B5289 and continue south for about 2 km.

Location 3 (163183) is the small parking area near Hause Point. Allow half an hour here, near the southern fault-bounded edge of the aureole.

Dark **tourmaline**, contrasting with the bleached hardened slates, has replaced the rock in places. Good samples can be collected from the old Rannergill lead trial 10 m along the road towards Hause Point. The vein resembles a black and white sandwich, trending due east.

Walk beside the wall away from the lake towards the bridge (168186) over Squat Beck. Small exposures and fallen boulders show uncleaved slump folds, small folds with **axial plane cleavages** and boudinage in sandstone beds, especially in the first 150 m from the roadside. As you look back towards the lake the convex slopes of the Rannerdale alluvial fan show up clearly. Across the lake is the **roche moutonnée**, Low Ling Crag (157183). A bar of gravel ties it to the 'mainland' beneath High Ling Crag (155182), below Mellbreak.

We now leave the turbidites of the northern sequence of the Skiddaw Group for the severely disrupted southern sequence, with its large slump masses up to 500 m long. Continue south to Buttermere village.

Location 4 (173169) is the coach and car park with public toilets and refreshment facilities behind the Bridge Hotel. A charge is made for parking. Allow 45 minutes for the geology.

Proceed to the viewpoint above the church. Figure 9.2 is a field sketch, showing Sour Milk Gill cascading out of its **hanging valley** and identifying the rock types which crop out. Follow the Buttermere

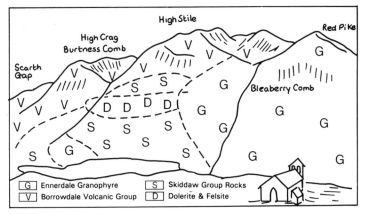

Figure 9.2 A field sketch of the High Stile ridge viewed from above Buttermere Church.

Formation exposures downhill (slowly, or you will miss much) to the bridge. Several, closely spaced, northeast–southwest trending, tight folds with minor folds on their flanks can be traced, especially by the doorstep of the Parish Room. Three phases of folding between Silurian and early Devonian times are present.

Walk back along the road to the small quarry (173173) where the slates are finely **cross** and **parallel laminated**. These colour banded rocks dip steeply southeast, as **sole** and **flute marks** show. Prominent cleavages and narrow quartz veins can be seen along the roadside. Drive on 3 km to the foot of the Honister Pass.

Location 5 (195150) is a car park, no longer free and often full, just beyond Gatesgarth Farm. This circuit is rough walking, so allow four hours. Follow the track below Fleetwith Pike into marshy Warnscale Bottom. Above and to our left is Low Raven Crag, where resistant sandstones show steeply inclined structures. This is possibly an olistolith, a detached raft of sandstone within generally finer-grained rocks, all part of the large northwest-directed submarine slide of the Buttermere Formation. Continue along the track until the ground steepens. Bear half-right at the first ruin, along a path leading into the lower waterfall complex.

Location 6 (201135) is the faulted rock junction in a plunge pool near a large rowan on the near or northern bank of Warnscale Beck. Fine-

73

grained slates of the Buttermere Formation downstream are tightly folded, showing graded bedding with more massive volcanic rocks upstream.

Return to the main path, the Pony Trod, down which slate was carried. Underfoot are fine samples of colourful amygdaloidal lavas, with crystals weathering out in places. Have a rest where the track enters the gorge of Warnscale Beck. Thin beds of lavas and tuffs dipping steeply southeast are exposed. Behind you is the straight-sided glaciated valley with its trough end and lakes, flanked by the massive, near vertical, volcanic crags of Haystacks to the south. The falls and plunge pools reflect differences in the hardness of the lavas and tuffs. Continue up the track.

Location 7 (208134) is the old Dubs Quarry buildings, overlooking the small marshy corrie and roches moutonnées of Dubs Bottom. The staircase-like descent of Warnscale Beck is evident, with the gorge separating the corrie from the longer, flatter section in Warnscale Bottom, the trough end. Walk along the old tramway path towards Honister for 300–400 m before turning left through a defile along a track on slate waste. This leads into the main Honister Quarry surface workings.

Location 8 (214137) is Hopper Quarry, now a partly filled area to the north of the track. A fault plane with mineralized **slickensides** can be traced for about 20 m at the southern edge of the quarry. Green tuffs with graded bedding are also clearly developed here.

In poor weather weak or inexperienced parties should retrace their footsteps. Otherwise, follow the rather indistinct path at the north end of Hopper Quarry past two small tarns to the top of Fleetwith Pike (205142). In this section small slabs with clasts standing out and the general southeasterly dip of the volcanics show up well. There is a clear contrast between the rounded tops of Skiddaw Group fells like Dale Head and the scalloped relief of the volcanic rocks of the High Stile ridge.

Carefully descend the steep arête of Fleetwith Edge, with its four rock steps.

Location 9 (202144) is near the base of the second rock step where you pass from Borrowdale Volcanic Group to Skiddaw Group rocks. The surface now becomes more friable and the beds thinner. This boundary is an **unconformity**, marked by a **conglomerate** between the two rock Groups which occurs on both sides of the Edge, between Striddle and Raven Crags.

10 · Glacial Features at Rosthwaite in Borrowdale

Ken Bond *formerly Exploration Manager with the Burmah Oil Company, Past President and former general Secretary of the Cumberland Geological Society*

PURPOSE

To view the glacial features near Rosthwaite. Additional short excursions to Skiddaw Group and Borrowdale Volcanic Group exposures are suggested.

PRACTICAL DETAILS

A half-day excursion. The extra locations recommended would extend it to a full day.

Drive from Keswick along either the west or east shores of Derwentwater, these roads joining at Grange. Rosthwaite, our starting point, is 3 km along the B5289 from Grange. It has a car park (257148) with public toilets, a village shop and a pub. Seatoller, 2 km further up the valley, has additional facilities including the only coach park in the valley but no pub. This is a walk of about 5 km on good paths at low levels around Rosthwaite. However suitable strong footwear is recommended.

os MAPS: 1:25 000 Outdoor Leisure Map, The English Lakes, North Western area

1:50 000, Sheet 89 or 90.

One inch (1:63 360), Touring Map No. 3, the English Lake District

GEOLOGICAL SETTING

Borrowdale covers 60 km² of spectacular scenery, combining high fells with soaring crags, steep woodlands of hardwood trees, with clear fast-flowing streams and flat meadows on the valley floors.

The junction between the Borrowdale Volcanic Group and the underlying Skiddaw Group sediments crosses the area from the west, near the south end of Derwentwater, and runs north to the east of the lake. The rounded fells to the north and west and the broad valley containing Bassenthwaite Lake are Skiddaw Group landscapes. The harder Borrowdale Volcanic Group rocks crop out on the steep cliffs and bare rocky surfaces further south in Borrowdale proper.

This excursion deals mainly with the most recent geological event, the Quaternary Ice Age, and the features left behind after the major ice retreat 18 000 years ago. Well-preserved glacial features around Ros-thwaite include large U-shaped valleys, dried-up lake beds, **kettle holes**, **roche moutonnées**, **terminal** and **lateral moraines** and ice-scoured surfaces.

EXCURSION DETAILS

There are three Parts: the road journey from Keswick to Rosthwaite, west of Derwentwater; the excursion proper, walking from Ros-thwaite; and the return to Keswick by road, east of Derwentwater.

Part 1

Follow the A66 west towards Cockermouth for 2 km, turn sharp left through Portinscale and follow the road signposted 'Grange'. After another 3 km this bends sharply, east of Cat Bells. From this viewpoint (248212), notice Walla and Falcon Crags, rising steeply above the eastern shores of the lake. These are **andesitic** block lava flows interbedded with **volcaniclastic** rocks, part of the Lower Borrowdale Volcanic Group.

After another 1.5 km stop briefly by a roadside seat (249195) or park by a roadside quarry (249197) overlooking the old Brandlehow lead mine. Dark blue or grey siltstones of the Kirkstile Slate Formation of the Skiddaw Group crop out on the fellside. These contain many steeply dipping veins of quartz with a rich suite of minerals. Brandlehow was worked before gunpowder was in general use and in the 1850s seventy to eighty men and boys worked here with a 10 m high waterwheel to drive the machinery. Samples of **galena** (the chief lead ore mined), **cerussite**, **sphalerite**, **fluorite**, **pyrite**, **barite** and quartz can be found in the overgrown tips below the road.

Continue south to Grange, crossing the river to join the B5289. The bridge foundations west of the river are built on a volcanic exposure forming a roche moutonnée. The glacier ice rounded and polished it, the deep scratches (striae) indicating the direction of flow.

Cross the bridge, turning right into the Jaws of Borrowdale where the River Derwent has cut a narrow gorge through particularly hard volcanic rocks. Castle Crag (249159), an isolated pinnacle, is prominent. When the ice was thickest it could have been a nunatak, a peak rising above the glacier. Continue for 3 km to Rosthwaite and turn right along a lane signposted 'Parking'.

Part 2

The map (Figure 10.2) gives the route and the locations we visit.

Rosthwaite nestles below a very large roche moutonnée, 'The How'. Turn right out of the car park, left at Yew Tree Farm, right again at Stone Croft, and go through a gate on to a field path signposted 'Longthwaite Youth Hostel'. Leave the path to reach the wall on the right at the top of a low hill. Location 1, an excellent viewpoint, is here.

The following summary of recent geological history after the end of the last glacial episode sets the scene.

When the glaciers started to retreat 18 000 BP (before present) only the highest Lake District peaks protruded above the ice. Vigorous valley glaciers had carved out the present U-shaped troughs and moved vast quantities of rock debris, which was deposited as sheets of drift, moraines, **drumlins**, etc as the glaciers retreated up their valleys. (Four stages of this retreat are shown in Figure 10.1 a–d.) Derwentwater and Bassenthwaite were one large lake with a glacier snout near Grange. This active glacier consisted of two tributaries from the Seathwaite and Stonethwaite valleys which joined south of Rosthwaite (see Figure 10.1a).

Rapid retreat continued, the Seathwaite glacier receding more quickly, until the situation was as represented in Figure 10.1b. A moraine at the entrance to the Jaws of Borrowdale ponded back a lake which extended up to Rosthwaite, where the Stonethwaite glacier completely blocked the valley, so that the Seathwaite valley drainage had to flow over or round the glacier snout. This glacier-dammed lake extended back almost to Seatoller. Another longer lake, dammed by a moraine at Thornythwaite (246134), stretched back to Seathwaite Farm.

As the Stonethwaite glacier retreated in three distinct phases, it left three concentric moraines near Rosthwaite before its snout retreated rapidly up the Stonethwaite and Langstrath valleys (see Figure 10.1c). The lake north of Rosthwaite broke through its morainic dam, draining away to leave marshy land. The outermost moraine of the Stonethwaite glacier blocked the valley so drainage water had to

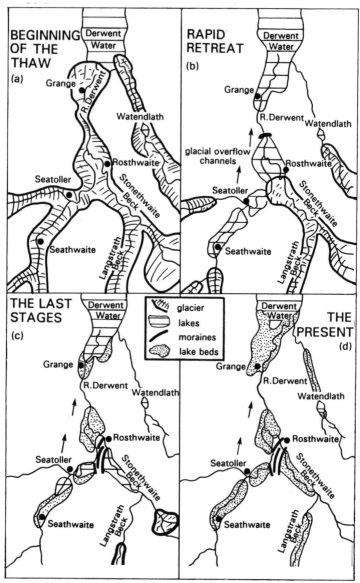

Figure 10.1 Recent glacial history south of Derwentwater showing:
(a) the beginning of the thaw; (b) rapid retreat; (c) the last stages;
(d) the present.

escape between the moraine and the fellside. Continued erosion cut through this and the Thornythwaite moraine, allowing the other two lakes to drain away.

As the Stonethwaite glacier continued its retreat, another lake formed behind the Rosthwaite moraines, extending up-valley almost to the rock barrier at Galleny Force (273131). This lake's outlet was on the east of the valley.

Today all the valley lakes above Derwentwater have drained away, although some old lake beds flood in wet weather. The moraines, except where cut by active streams, have resisted erosion and provide striking evidence of recent processes.

Location 1 (257146) is by the wall on top of the outermost or first moraine where it swings northeast into 'The How'. A smaller roche moutonnée is over the wall. Beyond, to the north, is the narrow gorge of the Jaws of Borrowdale with the isolated peak of Castle Crag. To the southwest the moraine continues as hummocky knolls to the river. Immediately southeast is the second or middle moraine, behind the last of the row of houses. The wide U-shaped Stonethwaite valley lies behind. Continue across the field to a stile. Turn left from the path to the wall.

Location 2 (258145) is by the wall on top of the middle and best preserved moraine and gives a good view southwest. This moraine heads towards some houses and reappears to their left as it swings towards the road. You should now return to the path, turning left through a gap in the wall which contains some very large erratic boulders. Join the road at Peat Howe, then turn right over the bridge to the Longthwaite Youth Hostel car park. From the stone seat in front of the youth hostel you can see the 5–7 m high ramparts of the second moraine. Follow the path south past the youth hostel to a rocky outcrop running down to the river.

Location 3 (254141) is the cleanly exposed, eroded face of the first moraine with its unsorted mixture of boulders, pebbles, sand, silt and clay. The river bends sharply here because ice forced it across to the west side of the valley. Water would have flowed over the glacier snout, cutting a channel first through the glacier and then through the terminal moraine once the ice melted. The hard volcanic rocks beside the footpath above the river have 'potholes' – smooth, rounded hollows – which could only have been formed by the scouring action of debris rotating in an eddy in stream rapids. These occur up to 5–7 m

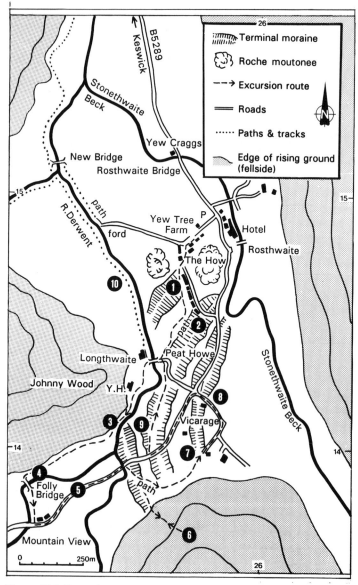

Figure 10.2 Excursion route and glacial features around Rosthwaite in Borrowdale.

above the present river, about the same height as the top of the moraine opposite. Continue along the path southwest from the rock outcrop on to the flat deposits of the old lake bed; and enter Johnny Wood, a National Trust oak woodland with luxuriant ferns and liverworts.

Location 4 (251139) is Folly Bridge, much in need of repair. Look at the eroded river bank with its exposure of typical, well-sorted lake bed sediments, silty material with some sand and small pebbles. Continue south to the houses, Mountain View (251137), on the main road and turn left towards Rosthwaite.

Location 5 (253138), 200 m northeast of Mountain View, gives an excellent view of the first moraine's rampart, crossing the valley almost at right angles, with a line of trees planted along its steeper southern side. Beyond this moraine, turn right through a gate along a path signposted 'Chapel Farm' and 'Borrowdale Church' into the hummocky ground and kettle holes of the southern end of the second moraine. Seek permission at Chapel Farm (258139) to make a diversion up the fellside, using the gate by the first moraine.

Location 6 (about 257137), on the fellside, gives an overview of the area. Return to the path, now a walled lane, near the farm.

Location 7 (258139) is at the end of the third or innermost moraine, which is only about 1–2 m high. Head north, to the right of a white building. Pass through the farm yard, where the ground level drops, confirming that considerable material was deposited between the moraines. Walk past the farm and Borrowdale Parish Church.

Location 8 (258142) is on the Stonethwaite road. Look across the flat lake beds to vestigial lateral moraines beyond Stonethwaite Beck. The B5289 runs north near the top of the third moraine. Continue to the crossroads and turn left (south) to join the path marked 'Rosthwaite'.

Location 9 (256141) is on the path along the top of the second moraine. Look at the profile and structure of the moraine. Follow the path to Peat Howe and either return directly to Rosthwaite or cross the bridge and turn north along the west bank of the River Derwent.

Location 10 (255146), on the river bank, offers a good view of the smaller roche moutonnée, with its smooth upstream slope and jagged, plucked, downstream slope. High on the west side of the valley the prominent Tongue Gill leads to quarry workings at Rigg Head, one of a line of quarries following the outcrop of a particularly good slate once extensively exploited. **Overflow channels** below High Doat (248144) and Castle Crag formed when the glacier level was very high. Cross the river at New Bridge (252151) and walk back to Rosthwaite over the flat former lake bed.

Part 3

Drive north along the B5289, initially crossing flat, low-lying fields, the former bed of the lake that existed in the early stages of ice retreat, see Figure 10.1b. A marker post to the right of the road indicates the possible depths of winter floods.

Follow the winding road through the gorge to the Bowderstone car park (254168). The quarry behind was previously known as 'Rainspot Quarry' because the regular splodges of dark material within the pale green andesite tuffs resemble rain spots. Nearby is the Bowder Stone, an enormous perched block of volcanic rock which either rolled down the crag or was carried by the ice.

Drive past the turning to Grange, with the actively growing 'crow's foot' delta of the River Derwent in front and to the left. If time permits take the very sharp right-hand turning by the Barrow Bay landing stage (269204) along the narrow road to Watendlath, extremely busy in high season. 'Surprise View' (269195), overlooking the Derwent delta, is one of many fine viewpoints. At Watendlath there is a fine **corrie** tarn behind a rock bar.

Return past the wooded knoll of Castle Head (269227), a **dolerite plug** that glaciers moulded to become a **crag and tail**. Chapter 13 describes this more fully.

11 · The Armboth Dyke, Thirlmere

From the original *by Morley Burton, Librarian, Cumberland Geological Society, with a contribution by Dr Steve Caunt*

PURPOSE

To trace the outcrop of the much-faulted Armboth **Dyke** with its distinctive rock which is so useful in showing the directions of ice movement.

PRACTICAL DETAILS

A half-day (4–5 hour) excursion. The 5 km walk over rough, boggy and sometimes steep land makes appropriate clothing and suitable strong footwear essential.

Access by car or minibus is along the narrow road to the west of Thirlmere. Start from the NWWA Armboth car park, with public toilets, at the foot of Fisher Gill (305172). The King's Head, Thirlspot (317177), is the nearest pub.

os MAPS: 1:25 000 Outdoor Leisure Map, the English Lakes, North Western area
1:50 000 Sheet 89 or 90
1:63 360 (One Inch) Touring Map No. 3, The English Lake District

GEOLOGICAL SETTING

The Armboth Dyke seems to be a vertical intrusion into the country rocks which are grey–green **tuffs** and coarse agglomerates (volcanic breccias of coarse angular fragments) of the Borrowdale Volcanic Group. The dyke outcrop, 2 km long and 5–10 m wide, extends from just south of the summit of Fisher Crag (305163) to near the head of Shoulthwaite Gill (294176) on the moorland of High Seat.

Seven **wrench** or **tear faults** shift the dyke outcrop sideways in its northwest-trending course. It formed later than the volcanic rock it intruded and may be related to the Threlkeld Microgranite, emplaced around 438 Ma during Ordovician times. If so, this was an early intrusive phase during the Caledonian **orogeny**.

The dyke rock is hard, rather pale, and very uniform in its composition with over 75% SiO_2 in the centre and 72% SiO_2 on its edges. Weathered, it is a brownish colour, sometimes with protruding quartz crystals, sometimes with hollows where these have weathered out. The centre is pink to brown in colour, the margins grey–green. The edges are fine-grained where the molten dyke material was chilled by contact with the country rock. The centre is **porphyritic** with big crystals or **phenocrysts** set in a fine-grained pink **feldspar** matrix. The phenocrysts are well-formed 2–3 mm transparent quartz and rectangular pink **orthoclase** crystals 1 cm or more in size. The soft material appearing as darkish patches is the mineral **chlorite**. Small chunky red glassy **garnets** can be found in the tuffs adjacent to the dyke. The garnets formed when the heat of the dyke baked the tuffs, a process known as contact metamorphism. The dyke does not form impressive topographic features, usually appearing as small rounded ice-scoured knolls and **roches moutonnées**. However its petrology is so different from the tuffs and its speckled appearance so distinctive that its outcrop can be easily traced.

The Thirlmere glacier carried dyke rock as far as the Shoulthwaite and Naddle valleys to the north and northwest, where it occurs as glacial **erratics**. However, fragments of dyke rock also occur on Armboth Fell and Wythburn Fell to the west and south, and perched blocks on crag tops 400 m west of Harrop Tarn at an altitude of about 550 m similarly suggest at least some ice flow to the south.

EXCURSION DETAILS

Numbered locations are shown on the accompanying map (Figure 11.1).

Begin at the NWWA car park north of Fisher Gill (305172). Follow the Watendlath footpath along the forest fence and up the steep zig-zags below Cockrigg Crags.

Location 1 (300168), just beyond the end of Cockrigg Crags, is a cairn of dyke rock. This is on a gentle slope by the large ash tree 20 m beyond the path's last zig-zag. The holes in the rocks are where quartz crystals have weathered out. The dyke stands out above the tuffs here.

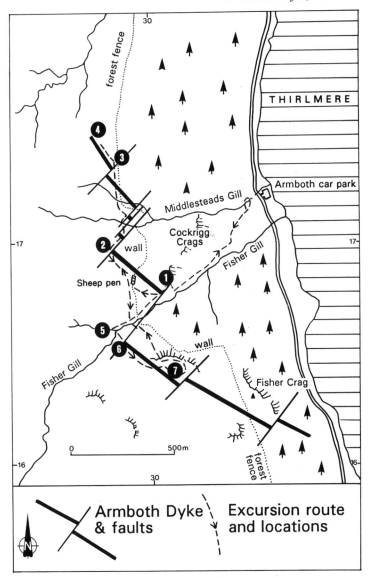

Figure 11.1 The Armboth Dyke, Thirlmere. (The dyke exposures are scattered and the fault positions are inferred.)

Climb northwestwards along the dyke above the path towards a wall and derelict sheep pen. Look for chunky red garnets in the thermally baked tuffs alongside.

Location 2 (298170) is 250 m to the northwest of the sheep pen where a wrench fault displaces the dyke 5–10 m to the right. This is conveniently marked by two circular rings of stones to the right of and below the outcrop. After another 50 m the dyke disappears due to faulting, with **slickensides** in the country rock just above. Walk 400 m north-northeast and then north across Middlesteads Gill, following the forest fence.

Location 3 (299173), an exposure of the dyke on a knoll 10–20 m from the plantation edge, shows many 5 mm long quartz crystals. **Jointed** and **cleaved** green tuffs of the Borrowdale Volcanic Group outcrop nearby.

Location 4 (298174) is 30–50 m to the northwest where marginal dyke rocks occur with fewer quartz but more orthoclase phenocrysts. Notice the close-set fractures and rounded weathered projections of the dyke. The dyke disappears under bracken and peat to the northwest. Its final outcrop in this direction is at a height of about 460 m just below the headwaters of Shoulthwaite Gill at (294176).

Return south-southeast to the wall and sheep pen beyond Location 2, then head south along the wall to its junction with the forest fence. Follow the Watendlath footpath southwest before dropping down to cross Fisher Gill.

Location 5 (298166) is a fresh exposure of volcanic tuffs in and along a small tributary near its confluence with Fisher Gill. They are deceptively similar in colour to the dyke rocks, possibly due to bleaching by organic acids derived from glacial drift or peat cover.

Location 6 (297164) is where the dyke reappears on a small knoll 50 m south of Fisher Gill. It has been shifted 400 m west of its outcrop at Location 1 to Locations 5 and 6 by wrench faulting, which also probably explains the course of Fisher Gill. Cross over flat boggy land 250 m southeastwards to the base of a ridge trending in the same direction.

Location 7 (301164) is an easily recognized outcrop of the dyke extending 50 m up the ridge to a smooth rocky knoll. As you approach this, the contrast between the pink dyke rock and the uniform greys of the volcanic tuffs shows up well. These tuffs display beautiful examples of banding and other sedimentary features exposed by weathering. The dyke continues southeast and there are some isolated exposures in the flat, very marshy ground towards Fisher Crag, inaccessible behind a forestry fence. Return to the Watendlath path, enjoying excellent views of Thirlmere and Raven Crag to the north, before descending to the car park along the rocky track below Cockrigg Crags.

12 · Quaternary features north of the Kirkstone Pass

Richard Clark *Cumberland Geological Society*

PURPOSE

To examine Pleistocene (mainly glacial) and Holocene (Recent) land forms and deposits north of the Kirkstone Pass, a main ice divide in the last glaciation.

PRACTICAL DETAILS

Either a full day's excursion or two comfortable half-day excursions on separate days.

Part 1 begins at the Cow Bridge car park (403134), and visits Dovedale. Part 2 starts from the Brotherswater Inn (404118) and is in higher, rougher country east of the A592. Not all the route is on regular paths. Appropriate, windproof clothing and suitable, strong footwear are essential for both excursions.

There are no public toilets, but there are hostelries with ample parking and toilets at the summit of Kirkstone Pass (401080), and the Brotherswater Inn on the A592. There are also several small roadside parking places.

Figure 12.1 is a sketch map of the area, showing the locations visited, and the route followed.

OS MAPS: 1:25 000 Outdoor Leisure Map, The English Lakes, North
             Eastern area
             1:50 000 Sheet 90

GEOLOGICAL SETTING

The country rocks belong to the Borrowdale Volcanic Group. Faults, master **joints** and crush lines control the patterns of main ridges,

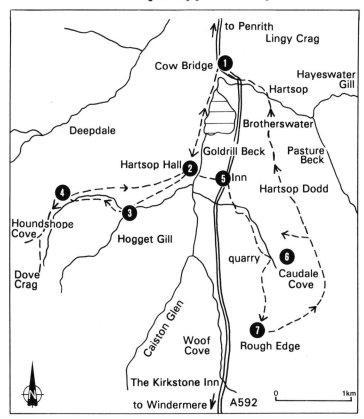

Figure 12.1 The excursion route north of the Kirkstone Pass.

valleys and many minor features. The crestline which forms the southern watershed probably corresponds generally with the zone of maximum local uplift in Late Tertiary–Early Pleistocene times. Today this crestline is an area of high precipitation. In glacial episodes it probably had heavy snowfall and was on the regional ice-shed, the divide on the surface of the ice cap.

Valley heads face north and valleys converge on the Ullswater trough. This major ice discharge route could not handle all the ice generated locally during the last glacial episode. Consequently ice deeply scoured the interfluves. Glacial erosion, including the deepening of the valleys, was cumulative during the Pleistocene Ice Ages. The area probably lost its last Upper Devensian ice cover before the warmer Windermere **Interstadial**, about 14 000–11 000 BP (before present). Severe climatic deterioration then led to the Loch Lomond **Stadial**, 11 000–10 000 BP, when valley and **corrie** glaciers waxed and waned for about 500 years. **Periglacial** conditions affected the much larger ice-free area and rivers carried much debris. This was a period of rapid landscape change.

The 10 000 years of the Holocene have experienced temperate climates. Deforestation and farming in the last few thousand years have accelerated movement of weathered material and eroded soils down to the valley floors and rivers.

EXCURSION DETAILS
Part 1

Figure 12.2 is a sketch section which shows the main features visited in this part of the excursion.

Location 1 (403 134) is Cow Bridge car park. Here Goldrill Beck follows the foot of the western valley wall. It has been displaced by the alluvial fan built on the valley floor by Hayeswater Beck which flows from the east. The apex of this fan is at the western edge of Hartsop hamlet. Old distributary channels can still be traced. The present stream course on the fan was embanked before the mid-eighteenth century to protect the open fields. Occasional floods still add coarse gravel to the fan, which was possibly initiated in the Upper Devensian but grew mainly during the Loch Lomond Stadial. Goldrill Beck has an artificial

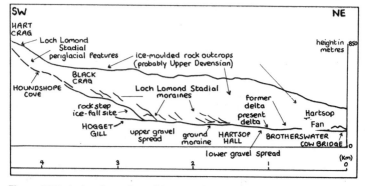

Figure 12.2 A sketch section of features between Cow Bridge and Hart Crag at the head of Dovedale.

course north of Cow Bridge, also to protect the open fields. Its previous **braided** courses ran northeast across the valley floor as far as fans built by other streams from the east.

A higher gravel bench at the eastern end of Hartsop was probably fed from the front of a shrinking Late Devensian valley glacier.

Notice the markedly ice-moulded crags (howes), along the foot of the eastern valley sides. Lingy Crag (411138) is partly scree-clad and its steep front is broken by rock failures. The plateau above this crag was much abraded by ice moving north. The prow of Grey Crag (426120) also has a slope failure site. Gullies and screes to the south are probably of Loch Lomond Stadial age, judging by their relationship to moraines in Pasture Beck valley (417123).

Follow the track south from the car park below the wood. Ice-moulded rock bosses on the hillside project through glacial **till**, scree and bedded slope materials. Brotherswater, which was probably impounded by the Hartsop fan, is shallow, unlike Ullswater with its ice-eroded rock basins.

The grassy flats by the southwest corner of the lake are the delta of Dovedale Beck, a stream diverted before the mid-eighteenth century to protect the open fields of High Hartsop (403118), a hamlet of which little now remains. The present stream course dates from the 1865 open field enclosure. The natural stream had previously built a gravel tongue down the centre of the valley with back-swamps on each side.

Location 2 (398120) is Hartsop Hall. Notice the ice-moulded outcrops across the valley near Sykeside (403118) with the gill and cove of Caudale (412108) above. High on the hillside, south of Caudale, are very old quarries.

The outermost **moraines** of the Dovedale (Loch Lomond Stadial) glacier lie between Hartsop Hall and its farm buildings. Follow the left, lower track, just beyond the buildings. The valley floor consists of **ground moraine**, very different from the gravel spreads upstream and downstream. A group of massive ice-transported boulders, incorporated in prehistoric earthworks (398117), is visible across the valley, below High Hartsop Dodd. Similar boulders are exposed in ground moraine on adjacent stream bluffs.

The track up Dovedale passes several morainic ridges which can be traced along the hillsides. These indicate glacier profiles at successive ice margins. Corresponding moraines on the south side of the valley are less prominent. The gravel of the wide upper valley floor was probably initially deposited by braided streams as the Loch Lomond Stadial glacier waned.

Location 3 (390114) is the confluence of Hoggett Gill with Dovedale Beck. The tributary stream, Hoggett Gill, joins Dovedale Beck just below a rock step in the main valley. The massive moraines mark the sites of the persistent ice margins of the active glacier in the main valley. Similar **recessional** moraines occur in Deepdale and Hayesdale. An ice-eroded rock step in Hoggett Gill is accessible over the footbridge just west of the confluence. Follow the path past the confluence, over the footbridge, and then turn uphill (right) on the path past the cascades over the rock step. Climb the stile, follow the line of an old fence and cross Dovedale Beck to the path north of the beck.

Location 4 (382116) is the group of morainic mounds below Black Crags. These moraines are probably the highest and youngest deposited by active ice in Dovedale. Follow the path from these mounds up to the valley head. This upper valley has interesting ice-moulded crags at Stangs (382112), rock-fall and debris trails below Dove Crag (376108) and periglacial features around Houndshope Cove (375113), reached by a steep climb north of Dove Crag.

Return to Hartsop Hall along the path north of Dovedale Beck, passing the old Hartsop lead mine (395118), worked from the seventeenth to the twentieth century. Proceed either to Cow Bridge, or follow the track across the valley floor from Hartsop Hall to Brotherswater Inn for Part 2.

Part 2

Figure 12.3 shows the route and the main features described.

Location 5 (404118), near the Brotherswater Inn, is where we begin. Gates east of the road near the inn and at Caudale Bridge give access to the fellside. Notice the ice-moulded howes south of the inn and how Caudale Beck has incised Upper Devensian tills. Follow the quarry sledge tracks up the sharp ridge south of the stream, from where it leaves its upper valley. Northward movement of the ice is indicated by north-pointing striae (scratches on the rock surface made by stones carried in moving ice) which can be seen on the path below the abandoned slate quarries.

Location 6 (412108) is Caudale Cove. Make your way carefully over quarry waste into the cove. The outermost moraine of a Loch Lomond Stadial corrie glacier and several recessional moraines can be

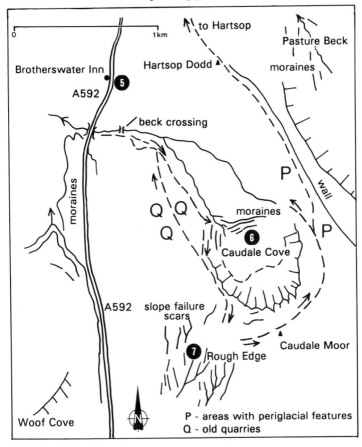

Figure 12.3 A sketch map showing Pleistocene and Holocene features around Caudale Cove, north of the Kirkstone Pass.

identified. Periglacial processes affected the headwall east and northeast of the corrie, while ice lingered in the southwest recesses of this cove.

There are many periglacial landforms on slopes north and east of Caudale Cove (especially above 600 m OD) and on Caudale Moor. These probably formed during the Loch Lomond Stadial and were added to during later episodes of excessively wet, snowy and cold weather such as the Little Ice Age of the seventeenth and eighteenth centuries. Most features are due to downslope flows of rock waste. The

93

thawed surface layer became saturated because water could not penetrate the underlying frozen ground and remained near the surface. Variations in wetness, composition and depth of the thawed layer influenced the speed and duration of debris movement. Differences in the rates of debris supply, steepness of slope and in successive pulses of movement helped to produce variety in landforms. The steep fronts of debris streams and sheets, which form straight or lobate banks across the hillsides, are the easiest to recognize. Look for flights of step-like features due to series of debris flows. Open joints truncated by the back wall of the cove have the same trend as the main valley and as slip scars on Rough Edge.

Location 7 (408095) is Rough Edge. Follow the ridge path above the quarries. Just above the steepest slope turn south along the hillside towards Rough Edge. This is an area of multiple rock failures with coherent rock slices above steep screes. The most recent movements were later than the last main glaciation. These failures may be due to a combination of causes. These include oversteepening of the valley sides, melting of the supporting glacier, water penetrating frost- and tension-opened joints parallel to the valley, and earth tremors. The many local failure sites younger than the Upper Devensian glacial maximum suggest that slope failure would have helped shape local relief throughout the Quaternary.

Woof Cove (398093), across the Kirkstone Pass, is a small, well-formed corrie with a marked lip, but unlike Caudale it lacks Loch Lomond Stadial moraines.

A complex of moraines extends alongside the A592 below Rough Edge for about 1 km south of Caudale Bridge. Their ages are uncertain but their location and large size suggest that at least the outermost date from the last stages of the main Upper Devensian glaciation.

To return, either retrace your footsteps or climb to Caudale Moor (414101), then walk north along the eastern rim of Caudale and descend into the cove to return to Brotherswater. To return to Cow Bridge, continue along the ridge past Hartsop Dodd. At (409126), where two walls 'vee' towards the summit, descend steeply to the right, following a well-marked path. Make for the east of Hartsop hamlet and continue to Cow Bridge.

13 · Landscape development near Keswick

John Boardman *Lecturer in Geography,*
Hertford College, Oxford

PURPOSE

To examine the evidence for glacial and **periglacial** processes in the
Keswick area.

PRACTICAL DETAILS

Allow 2–3 hours for this walk from the centre of Keswick, following
public footpaths over level but wet ground. Suitable strong footwear is
recommended. The most convenient car park is on Lake Road, next to
the Century Theatre.

OS MAPS: 1:25 000 Outdoor Leisure Map, The English Lakes, North
Western area

GEOLOGICAL SETTING

The Lake District has long been regarded as a classic area for
landforms and deposits resulting from glaciation. However the
evidence available is remarkably limited, almost all relating to the
most recent glaciation in the Devensian Stage. As illustrated by its
recent glacial history, the area has probably been affected by many
glacial episodes, although their character is debatable.

For perhaps 15 000 years of the Devensian Stage, from 30 000 to
15 000 years before the present (BP), an ice sheet covered most of
northern Britain, including very many Lake District peaks. When the
ice sheet was at its greatest extent there was probably very little
erosion beneath it.

At the end of this period and during the Loch Lomond **Stadial**
(11 000–10 000 BP), when small glaciers reappeared in the Lake

District, **corrie** and valley glaciers were active. Corries formed and developed and valleys were deepened at such times. However if such phases of ice movement in corries and valleys were brief, their overall impact on the landscape must have been limited. There is little evidence of the character and length of glacial episodes in the Lake District before the Devensian. All is conjecture.

Most of the evidence for glaciation is from deposits. Sediments may help dating if they contain usable material such as organic remains. Where erosion has been dominant, the sedimentary record is usually incomplete or relates only to the most recent events. As the sediments of the Keswick lowland are Devensian in age they tell us nothing of earlier glacial events. Where evidence is limited, the erosional history of an area is difficult to reconstruct, the northern Lake District being no exception. This excursion looks at sediments and landforms of Devensian age, and explores the questions they raise about earlier glacial history.

EXCURSION DETAILS

Figure 13.1 shows the features and locations visited.

Enter the National Trust property of Crow Park through the gate opposite the Lake Road car park exit. Walk the short distance to the top of the grassy hill.

Location 1 (263231) is this hill, an excellent example of a **drumlin**, one of many in the area. The street pattern of Keswick reflects the streamlined form of the drumlins upon which it is built. The Heads, on the drumlin just north of Hope Park Golf Course, illustrates this well.

Drumlins stream northwards from Keswick along the shores of Bassenthwaite and on to the Solway Plain. Some large examples can be identified on local OS maps by their oval-shaped enclosed contours. Drumlins were formed by moving ice with shear stresses at the base sufficient to mould soft sediments such as glacial **till** into streamlined bedforms. The crest lines of the drumlins suggest the directions of ice flow (see Figure 13.1). Ice probably moved from south to north, from the high ground of the central Lake District towards the Solway Plain and the Irish Sea Basin. Analyses of stone types in drumlins around Keswick confirm this inference. From Crow Park, continue along Lake Road past the landing stages.

Location 2 (263222) is Friar's Crag. This well-known viewpoint consists of **dolerite** whose contact with Skiddaw Group rocks can be

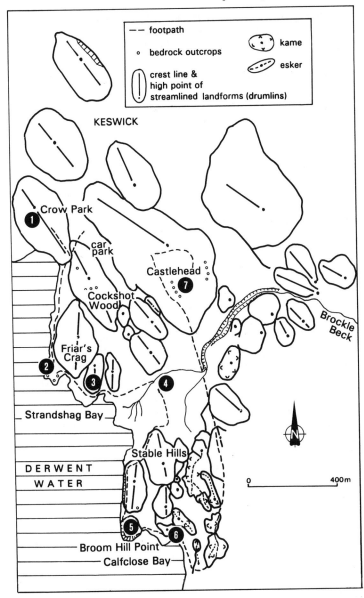

Figure 13.1 Glacial landforms of the Keswick area.

traced just above high water mark. At its southern end, a series of plaques, usually submerged, records low lake levels. The resistant dolerite appears to form the core of a drumlin whose up-glacier or stoss end has been eroded by lake waves. Such features are known as **crag and tail**. Dolerite outcrops also occur in Cockshot Wood and Castlehead, where they again form the core of streamlined glacial landforms. Between Friar's Crag and Strandshag Bay the path skirts the stoss ends of two drumlins.

Location 3 (265223) is the larger western drumlin. The relationship between the two drumlins can only be appreciated by walking over them and seeing them from different viewpoints. The smaller merges into the larger and may have been superimposed on to its flanks. It may represent a later, low-energy phase of glacial moulding with shear stresses insufficient to modify the earlier, larger forms. Drumlin sizes vary considerably in this area. The path continues through a wooded marshy area known as the Ings, the delta of Brockle Beck.

Location 4 (268223) is the footbridge in the wood where Brockle Beck is crossed. The high gravel banks confining the beck are rather an inefficient form of river control, as they deal with the symptoms rather than the causes of flooding. The problem seems to be the higher gradient section of the channel on steeper slopes east of the Borrowdale road at Bow Barn (271223). This section is now unstable, due to erosion of glacial and **glacifluvial** deposits releasing large amounts of gravel. Improved drainage, or change in land use leading to increased stream flow, are likely causes. As you leave the woodland, turn right along the track, following the base of a drumlin to Stable Hills (268218). There is an exposure of till along the lakeside in a long, low drumlin south of Stable Hills.

Location 5 (267215), Broom Hill Point, is a better exposure. It is the eroded remnant of another drumlin whose interior is bouldery till, best seen from the lakeshore. Measurements of the preferred orientations of elongated stones from this site show that their long axes lie parallel to the direction of ice movement. This can be confirmed independently from orientations of drumlin crest lines in the area.

The till is extremely tough and difficult to disaggregate. Use a knife to prod the zone between 0.5 and 1.0 m below the surface. The high bulk density of the till is not an original feature. It is likely to be the result of later repeated freezing and thawing of the ground in the periglacial conditions of a tundra-like climate 10 000–11 000 years ago. This is known as a **fragipan** or a **fragic** horizon. Such horizons are widespread in many highland areas, where they make drainage difficult, impede root penetration, and cause tree windthrow. Follow the path alongside Calfclose Bay.

Location 6 (270215) is a low ridge, to the left, in the field. Material exposed in molehills and in the banks of a small stream suggests that this ridge consists of sand and gravel. It is loose and better sorted than the clayey till at Broom Hill Point. The ridge is one of several in the vicinity which are low **eskers** or glacier crevasse infills. Meltwater flow beneath or among stagnating blocks of ice formed these features, which represent the final phase of glaciation when the ice had ceased to move. This type of landscape, dominated by sand and gravel features such as **kames** and eskers, is known as 'ice stagnation topography'.

Walk back towards Keswick along the path beside Borrowdale Road, noticing the low sand and gravel ridges in the field west of the road. Make a detour to climb Castlehead.

Location 7 (269227) is Castlehead, the main outcrop of the dolerite previously seen at Friar's Crag. The contrasts between the landscapes of the Skiddaw Group and the Borrowdale Volcanic Group rocks can be seen clearly from the summit. The often precipitous slopes east of Borrowdale and the craggy topography of the Scafell area to the south are developed on the massive, resistant and rather varied volcanic rocks.

North and west of the Derwent Water–Bassenthwaite valley, including the Skiddaw massif, the rock is mainly thinly **cleaved** mudstone or slate, with occasional sandstone beds. Frost rapidly breaks down the slates to form a thick covering of scree on the slopes. Thornthwaite Forest and Dodd Wood, on either side of Bassenthwaite, grow in soils developed on scree. This is over 10 m deep in places at the foot of long slopes like Dodd Wood and Latrigg. There are many scree exposures along forestry roads, with a particularly fine one by the roadside at Throstle Shaw (237272). Thus the main reason for smooth slopes on Skiddaw Group rocks is that the thick cover of frost-shattered material hides irregularities. Most of this material is a legacy from the final periglacial phase of the last ice age which ended 10 000 years ago. Today frost shatter is ineffective in the Lake District, even at high altitudes.

Castlehead has a long tail of till on its northwest or down-ice flank. This is a common feature in the lee of resistant rock outcrops. From the summit much of Borrowdale and its northerly continuation containing Bassenthwaite can be seen. This is traditionally regarded as a glaciated valley, though the evidence can be interpreted differently. Derwent Water occupies a rock basin which may be a typical glacial feature. Its maximum depth is 22 m, whereas Bassenthwaite Lake (19 m deep) seems to be dammed by glacial debris which changed the course of the Derwent from its pre-Devensian route along the Embleton valley to a more northerly course. The presence of **hanging valleys** is often quoted as evidence for significant glacial erosion of an area. From Castlehead, the Watendlath valley is seen to 'hang' over Borrowdale, the Lodore Falls being at the steep descent of Watendlath Beck into Borrowdale.

Geological controls are important here, as they are in many hanging valley relationships. The deeper excavation of the Derwent Water–Bassenthwaite valley is due to its location on the less resistant Skiddaw Group slates and is just as likely to be due to pre-glacial river erosion as to glaciation. Hanging valleys are few in the Lake District.

At Grange the valley widens into a steep-sided trough, typical of the textbook glaciated valley. This occurs at precisely the point where the river leaves the volcanic rocks for the Skiddaw Group. Some slight overdeepening by glacial processes produced the rock basin in which Derwent Water lies but the evidence overwhelmingly suggests a pre-glacial river system which suffered minimal glacial modification.

Castlehead overlooks the excursion route. The distinction between the larger-scale forms due to glacial streamlining and the smaller features due to ice stagnation can be appreciated here. Return to Keswick by crossing the road at the foot of Castlehead to follow the footpath towards Cockshot Wood between the drumlins. The path skirts the base of Cockshot Wood, leading directly to the Lake Road car park.

For further details of the geomorphology of the Keswick area, refer to: Boardman, J. (1982) Glacial Geomorphology of the Keswick Area, Northern Cumbria, *Proc. Cumberland Geol. Soc.*, 5, 115–134. For more general information, refer to: Boardman, J. (1988), see Further Reading (p. 146).

14 · The Skiddaw Granite north of Threlkeld

Tom Shipp *Past President and former General Secretary, Cumberland Geological Society*

PURPOSE

To examine the Skiddaw Granite exposure in Sinen Gill; to notice how the granite has **thermally metamorphosed** rocks of the Skiddaw Group; and to visit old lead and copper mine workings nearby.

PRACTICAL DETAILS

A whole day excursion, with about 7 km to walk, mainly over bleak, rough, boggy moorland rising to 500 m. Appropriate windproof clothing and suitable strong footwear are recommended.

Turn off the A66 into Threlkeld village (3225), where you take the road signposted 'Blease Road leading to Blencathra', which is narrow and unsuitable for coaches. Follow this road to our starting point, the car park (302257), just past and above the Blencathra Centre. Threlkeld has pubs and a shop.

OS MAPS: 1:25 000 Outdoor Leisure Map, English Lakes, North Western area
1:50 000 Sheet 89 or 90

GEOLOGICAL SETTING

There are three separate outcrops of the greyish-white Skiddaw Granite in an extensive area of dark-coloured, thermally metamorphosed Skiddaw Group mudstones and **greywackes**. The map (Figure 14.1) shows these locations. We visit the southern exposure in Sinen Gill (302282), near the headwaters of the Glenderaterra Beck.

The thermal metamorphism of an area of about 70 km^2 of Skiddaw Group rocks suggests that the granite outcrops are connected not far below the surface. The metamorphosed area extends east to west from Bowscale Fell to Skiddaw, and north to south from Coomb Height to Lonscale Fell (see Figure 14.1). This small intrusion is probably a stock, steep-sided and flat-topped. Evidence from **gravity anomalies** indicates that relatively light rock underlies the area, part of the **batholith** extending beneath the Northern Lake District and the Northern Pennines. **Radiometric** age determinations of the Skiddaw Granite give a mean of 399 +/− 6 **Ma**, suggesting late Silurian or early Devonian emplacement, almost at the end of the **Caledonian orogeny**.

The granite consists of interlocking crystals of white, rectangular **orthoclase** and **oligoclase** (a **plagioclase**) feldspar, dark, platy **biotite** mica and glassy, grey quartz. The northern outcrop has been extensively altered to **greisen** (where the feldspars have been replaced by silvery flakes of gilbertite, a variety of **muscovite** mica). This is a **metasomatic** process, caused by chemically active fluids migrating through the rock. The presence of minerals containing additional fluorine, silica and water absent from the 'normal' granite as well as mineral veins passing from the greisen into surrounding rocks is evidence of these chemically active fluids. The Sinen Gill granite has a higher ratio of plagioclase to orthoclase than the granite of the central outcrop. It could be classified as a biotite-**granodiorite.**

The granite intruded mudstones and greywackes of the Skiddaw Group, already mildly **regionally metamorphosed** earlier in the Caledonian orogeny. The metamorphic **aureole** extends outwards from the granite exposures and many attempts have been made to map and interpret various stages of alteration within the aureole.

Field observations suggest three stages of thermal metamorphism:

(a) an outer, mildly metamorphosed area, with white **chiastolite** crystals and occasional dark spotting of the slightly hardened mudstones;

(b) an intermediate area of much hardened and **hornfelsed** slate or mudstone with dull black spots of **cordierite**;

(c) an inner zone, closest to the granite, where alteration by heat has produced tough, well-crystallized hornfels, with black spots of cordierite having a pitchy lustre, and transparent **andalusite porphyroblasts.**

There are no clearly defined metamorphic zones. As you get nearer to the granite the hornfels becomes increasingly crystalline, with the metamorphic minerals and textures becoming easier to recognize.

There is extensive mineralization with lead and copper-bearing veins following faults and lines of weakness in the country rocks.

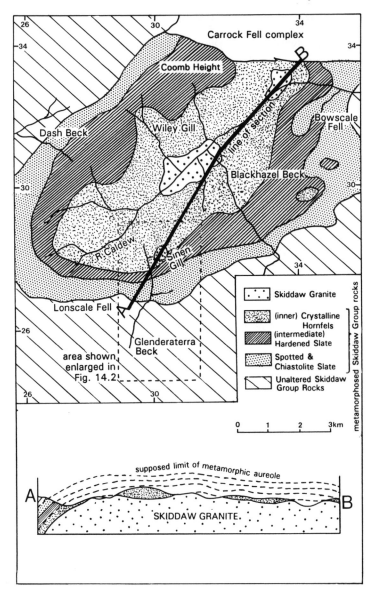

Figure 14.1 A geological sketch map and section of the Skiddaw Granite area.

EXCURSION DETAILS

Figure 14.2 shows the route followed and locations visited. Begin from the car park above the Blencathra Centre (302257) and head west-northwest along the rough cart track.

Location 1 is the exposure of hardened blue–grey Skiddaw Group mudstones above this track, opposite the end of the Centre's boundary wall. These show the effects of regional, not thermal, metamorphism. Follow the upper track around the lower slopes of Blease Fell and examine nearby boulders and small exposures for the beginning of thermal metamorphism (ill-defined grey spotting in the rocks). Many exposures show a dark sheen and hardening of the slate.

Location 2 (299270) is at the first gill, below a waterfall 1.5 km from the start. There is much reddening of the rock and spectacular development of white, randomly orientated chiastolite crystals. This gill could be fault guided. Continue along the track to a bridge over Roughten Gill.

Location 3 (298276) is here at Roughten Gill. The bridge is made of flat slabs of hardened hornfels containing the dark cordierite of the intermediate stage of contact metamorphism. One of the slabs is a 'misfit' of green volcanic slate. There are also a few boulders of white Skiddaw Granite. The hornfels slabs ring when tapped *gently* with a hammer. *Please do not damage by hammering.*

Head northeast from Roughten Gill for 0.5 km across rising, boggy moorland to Sinen Gill and follow it upstream.

Location 4 (301282) is a prominent waterfall, where strongly **jointed**, weathered granite is exposed. Continue upstream.

Location 5, at the next waterfall, is the granite–hornfels contact, here with a low angle of dip. Proceed another 0.3 km upstream.

Location 6 (304283) is near a ruined sheepfold north of the stream. Just below this an exposure of hornfelsed greywackes shows relict small-scale folds with **axial planar cleavage**. These structures are best seen on the weathered rock faces. Did the folding with axial-plane cleavage precede or post-date the thermal metamorphism? *No hammering of the rock faces, please.* Return downstream past the waterfall at Location 4.

Location 7 is an outcrop where the granite on the south bank of the gill has been deeply weathered and **kaolinized**. Peaty acids may have accelerated decomposition of the feldspars, as joints in the granite are filled with black and brown, structureless, carbonaceous material.

Descend to the confluence of Sinen Gill with Glenderaterra Beck and then turn south towards Roughten Gill. A mineral vein with abundant gossan (iron stained quartz) crosses the beck, and was worked from a small, now collapsed **adit**.

Location 8 (297275) is at the confluence of Roughten Gill and Glenderaterra Beck, where small specimens of vivid green **malachite** and brassy **chalcopyrite** may be found below a prominent vein. Carry on downstream, past two more collapsed adits.

Location 9 (296272) is the ruined Glenderaterra Mine on the opposite

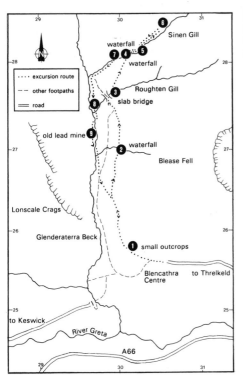

Figure 14.2 A sketch map of the excursion route to the Skiddaw Granite in Sinen Gill.

Figure 14.3 The remains of the Glenderaterra Mine (Location 9). *Photo*: T. Shipp

(west) bank (see Figure 14.3). *Take care. One shaft is open and flooded.* Abundant specimens of heavy, white, platy crystals of **barite**, white crystals of quartz (often mimicking barite), grey, heavy **galena** with a silvery sheen when freshly broken and pale yellow incrustations of **pyromorphite** can be collected here.

Re-cross Glenderaterra Beck where there used to be a bridge, walk steeply uphill to the right, to the higher track, and so back to the car park.

15 · The Carboniferous Limestone between Caldbeck and Uldale

Tom Shipp *Past President and former General Secretary, Cumberland Geological Society*

PURPOSE

To examine part of the Carboniferous Limestone succession on the northern edge of the Lake District.

PRACTICAL DETAILS

A half-day excursion. It could become part of a whole day excursion, 'the round of Skiddaw', by car, minibus or coach from Keswick via Mungrisdale, Hesket Newmarket, Caldbeck, Uldale, Castle Inn at Bassenthwaite, and back to Keswick.

Caldbeck village has a pub, shops and public toilets. Parking is available on roadside verges and in laybys near the locations described, which are all close to the roadside, on open moorland and freely accessible. Suitable, strong footwear is advised. *Be careful in the old quarries where safety helmets should be worn.*

OS MAPS: 1:50 000 Sheets 85 and 90 (Sheet 85 shows Locations 1 and 2, Faulds Brow and Old Quarries; Sheet 90, Locations 3 and 4, Aughertree Fell and Green How)

BGS MAP: 1:50 000 Sheet 23 (Cockermouth), Solid or Drift edition

GEOLOGICAL SETTING

The tilted, dissected plateau just north of Caldbeck and Uldale consists of limestones, sandstones and shales of Lower Carboniferous age which dip gently northwest away from the Lake District. Carrock Fell stands out boldly to the south, while the summit ridge of Skiddaw, seen end-on, dominates the view to the southwest.

Outcrops of Carboniferous Limestone, which occur as fault blocks

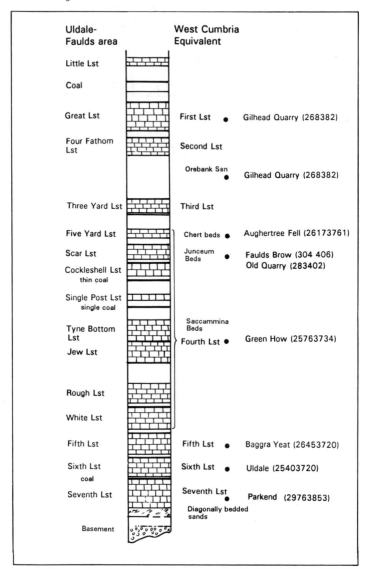

Figure 15.1 The Carboniferous Limestone succession in the Caldbeck to Uldale area with West Cumbrian equivalents. The map references show the positions of selected quarries in the sequence.

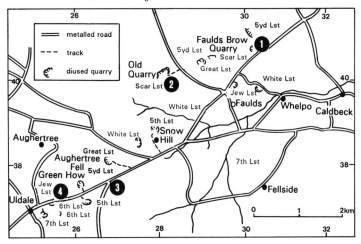

Figure 15.2 Map of the area between Uldale and Caldbeck. (Adapted from *Proc. Cumberland Geol. Soc.*, 4, Part 1, 49, with permission.)

dipping radially outwards, almost completely surround the Lake District. These rocks vary greatly in their nature, the Caldbeck area showing a **lithology** transitional between the Lower Carboniferous of West Cumbria and that of the Alston Block of the North Pennines. The West Cumbrian limestone units thin to the northeast, with intervening shales and sandstones becoming thicker. This is because conditions became more estuarine northeastwards, with occasional lobes of deltaic sediments being deposited in the Carboniferous seas, followed by uplift and subaerial erosion. The Yoredale succession of the Pennines shows this pattern of repeated deposition best with limestone–sandstone–shale–**cyclothems** showing the upward passage from open sea to delta-top swamp forest conditions.

The Caldbeck–Uldale lithology suggests entirely marine environments, without the full cyclothem sequence. Figure 15.1 shows the geological succession in the area. The map (Figure 15.2) shows the four locations described and other sites worth a visit if time allows.

EXCURSION DETAILS

Start from the car park (323399) by the river in Caldbeck. Drive northwestwards out of Caldbeck village along the road signposted to Carlisle. This climbs steeply over a downfaulted block of Namurian shales and sandstones, with long-abandoned coal workings in the

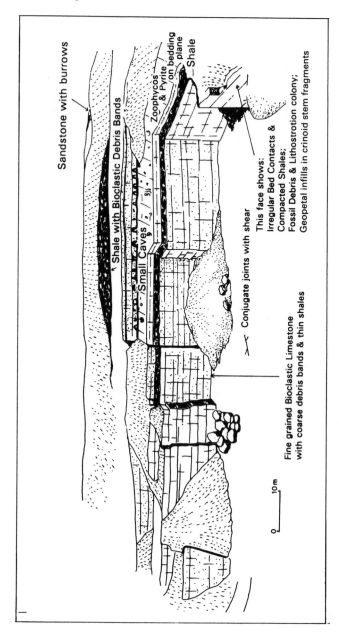

Sandstone with burrows

Shale with Bioclastic Debris Bands

Zoophycos & Pyrite on bedding plane — Shale

'Small Caves

This face shows:
Irregular Bed Contacts &
Compacted Shales;
Fossil Debris & Lithostrotion colony;
Geopetal infills in crinoid stem fragments

Conjugate joints with shear

Fine grained Bioclastic Limestone
with coarse debris bands & thin shales

0   10m

Figure 15.3 Field sketch of Faulds Brow Quarry. All the sequence is readily accessible, but the quarry faces are loose and dangerous. (Adapted from *Proc. Cumberland Geol. Soc.*, 5, Part 2, 132–3, copyright © Kershaw and Gaudoin.)

rough, gorse-covered ground to the left of the road. Turn left (southwestwards) at the crossroads at the top of the hill 2 km from Caldbeck and follow the minor road for 1.5 km.

Location 1 (304406), Faulds Brow Quarry, is to the right of the road. It is in the Scar Limestone, Brigantian in age and equivalent to part of the Fourth Limestone of West Cumbria (see Fig 15.1) and within the Chief Limestone Group of northern England. Figure 15.3 is a field sketch of this quarry, which was worked for roadstone along a bedding plane dipping 12° west-southwest. The main wall here is a 7 m thick, pale grey, compact limestone bed with widely spaced bedding planes and strong **joints**. Fossils are few; only crinoid and **rugose** coral fragments.

Enter the upper quarry along grass or earth slopes at its left-hand (western) end. *Do not climb the quarry face, as the rock has been loosened by explosives.* Compact, grey, granular limestone with rusty weathering nodules of **pyrite** can be seen on the floor of a shallow embayment at the left-hand end of the upper face. All the limestones of this quarry are strongly jointed with percolating groundwater staining joint blocks to a depth of several centimetres. Solution and precipitation of calcite has also occurred along joints.

The walls of this embayment consist of 1 m of grey, rather gritty limestone, with some crinoids and solitary corals (notably *Aulophyllum*) passing upwards into 0.4 m of dark, crumbly shale. Fragments of crinoids, solitary and colonial corals, small brachiopods, **bryozoa** and the very occasional trilobite can be found in this shale which merges upwards into coarse, fragmental limestone.

Move several metres to the right up to an area loosened by shot-firing. Curious, spiral, fan-like markings of the **trace fossil**, *Zoophycos*, can be seen on weathered bedding planes. These markings are thought to be feeding burrows of an unidentified marine organism. The abundant pyrite and the trace fossils suggest a low-energy marine environment, with stagnant, probably shallow, water. Scramble carefully 2 m down on to the main upper bench of the quarry. The upper 2 m of limestone were worked here along a joint plane covered with calcite dripstone. The second set of joints can be seen as thin, vertical cracks almost at right angles to the face. A thin, impermeable shale underlies the limestone face, whose joints open into small 'burrows', 10–20 cm in diameter, just above the shale. This is a joint-aligned solution network, a cave system in miniature (see Figure 15.4). The floor of this part of the quarry, a gently undulating bedding plane, can be envisaged as having been part of a tropical sea floor in

Figure 15.4 Solution cavities associated with jointing in limestone, Faulds Brow Quarry. *Photo*: T. Shipp

Carboniferous times. Small raised coral colonies, including *Lithostrotion* and *Syringopora* (see Figure 1.4a and c), can be found here.

The quarry opens northwards on to moorland. Beds of dark grey, fossiliferous shale and overlying pale brown sandstone with fossil burrows have been removed and dumped near the quarry entrance. This spoil contains good specimens of the 'Ram's Horn' coral, *Zaphrentis*, small brachiopods, crinoid stems and plates.

From Faulds Brow Quarry proceed southwestwards for 1 km to a crossroads, turn right and continue for another 1 km. Then follow the track west, by the sign 'Caldbeck Common. No Tipping', to a roofless workshop.

Location 2, Old Quarry (283402), is beyond this building and lies just east of Seat (344 m). Its limestone and shale succession is similar to that at Faulds Brow but with differing thicknesses. There are several bioherms, oval reef-like mounds of coarse shelly debris, as illustrated in Figure 15.5. Return to the crossroads and travel 4 km southwest along the Uldale road.

Location 3 (268377) is Aughertree Fell. Stop at any convenient layby and investigate the moorland south of the road. The numerous depressions up to 10 m deep in the moorland are sink holes in limestone blanketed by peat and soil cover. Their alignment suggests they may follow major joint intersections or faults. Continue southwest along the road for 1 km to where it crosses Green How (258373), then walk north to grassed-over spoil heaps 200 m or so from the road.

This long-disused quarry is in the Jew and Tynebottom Limestones, where the sequence is not easy to follow. At the base, 2 m or so

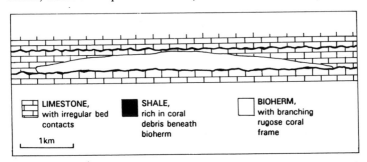

Figure 15.5 Outline of a small patch reef at Old Quarry (5.7 m above base). Note the thinning of the limestone bed above the reef. (Adapted from *Proc. Cumberland Geol. Soc.*, 5, Part 2, 136, with permission.)

of pale grey limestone with reddish spots contain the coral *Lonsdaleia* and the large brachiopod *Gigantella*; 6 m of well-bedded, splintery limestone come next with *Saccaminopsis*, a small bead-like **foraminiferid**, and the corals *Aulophyllum*, *Dibunophyllum* (see Figure 1.4d) and *Nemistium*. Higher up is a 15 cm thick **marker band** containing the compound coral, *Lithostrotion phillipsi*. A 1 m thick, dark-coloured limestone band, containing the rugose coral, *Caninia*, forms the top of the succession. *Please do not hammer the face* – specimens can be collected from the sparse debris below.

There are many more old quarries and diggings in this area, as the sketch map (Figure 15.2) shows. For further details, refer to: Shackleton, E. H. (1978) The Carboniferous Limestones of the area around Caldbeck and Uldale, *Proc. Cumberland Geol. Soc.*, 4, Part 1, 46–50; and Kershaw, S. and Gaudoin, D. (1989) The Scar Limestone at Faulds Brow Quarry, Caldbeck, Northern Lake District, *Proc. Cumberland Geol. Soc.*, 5, Part 2, 129–149.

16 · The Penrith Sandstone of the Vale of Eden

Jim Cockersole *Past President, Cumberland Geological Society*

PURPOSE

To study the dune and **brockram facies** of the Lower Permian Penrith Sandstone and their environments of deposition.

PRACTICAL DETAILS

Two one-day excursions are described. Excursion 1 is in the area north of Penrith, studying the aeolian (wind-blown) dune facies of the Penrith Sandstones and including one exposure of the brockram. There is a total of 2–3 km walking at the widely spaced locations, so a vehicle is essential.

Excursion 2 visits the Appleby and Brough areas, examining both the dune and brockram facies. As a vehicle can approach close to all locations, little walking is involved.

In general, parking is possible and safe at the roadside. The walking is easy and generally on footpaths and enclosed land. Locations may be accessible from rights-of-way or by permitted access. Users are asked not to abuse the right of access to these sites and to seek permission if in any doubt. Several locations are SSSIs, so *please don't hammer!*

OS MAPS: 1:50 000 Sheets 90 (Locations 1–4), 86 (Locations 5–6), 91 (Locations 7–10)
1:25 000 Sheet NY 43/53 (Locations 1–4)
BGS MAP: 1:50 000 Penrith, Sheet 24, Solid

GEOLOGICAL SETTING

These excursions study the Penrith Sandstone Formation of the Eden Valley, which was deposited in an elongated Permo-Triassic basin

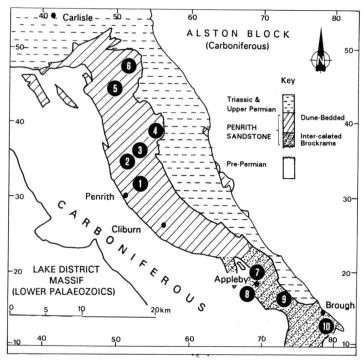

Figure 16.1 The Permo-Triassic rocks of the Vale of Eden.

lying between the Pennines and Lake District mountains. These Lower Permian desert sandstones accumulated as wind-blown deposits in a Sahara-like dune field in the centre of the basin. Marginal alluvial facies consist of brecciated material brought down by flash floods from the surrounding highlands. In places these coarse deposits, the brockrams, interfinger with the dune sandstones.

Figure 16.1 is a geological map of the area showing the Permo-Triassic outcrops and the locations visited.

The Dune Deposits

The most striking feature of the sandstone is the large-scale **cross-bedding** which indicates its origin as ancient desert dunes. The concave foreset beds dip consistently at up to 30° to the northwest. They were formed by wind-blown sand accumulating on the steep leading slopes of advancing dunes, as illustrated in the photograph

(Figure 16.2). Each dune foreset unit is separated from overlying units by a low-angle plane of erosion, a bounding surface. This shows that the top of the lower dune had been removed before the later one advanced over it, as illustrated in the other photograph (Figure 16.3). These units are the basal remnants of crescentic dunes, originally about 25 m high and 200 m long, which migrated in front of winds blowing from the east or northeast in Permian times.

The Brockram Facies

Especially near the southern end of the depositional basin, the wind-blown sandstones pass laterally into water-lain, flat-bedded sandstones and **breccias**, the 'brockrams'. **Alluvial fans** along the basin edges were half-cone-shaped masses of sediment, largely of southerly derivation. These were deposited by flash floods that swept down from highlands to the south. After flowing through narrow **wadis**, the streams split into distributaries when they reached the basin. These spread the stream load over the surfaces of the fans. The poorly sorted sediments show a rapid decrease in particle size downstream and there was reworking of material by **braided** streams. On the flood plain and in the basin these processes resulted in flat-bedded fluvial sandstones with occasional playa (temporary lake) deposits and the interfingering of fluvial and dune sandstones. Locations 6 and 10 best illustrate these features.

Excursion 1

Location 1 (542309), the disused Cowraik Quarry, is a good starting point. It is situated on Beacon Edge, near a minor road which links the A6 and the A686 across the northern outskirts of Penrith. The quarry is a local nature reserve classified as an SSSI by English Nature, which has produced a leaflet describing the geological features. Enter along a footpath leading up from the road (540308).

The quarry has upper and lower levels, with rough tracks giving access to old faces which show the large-scale cross-stratification of dune-bedded sandstones. It is best to visit in winter or spring before plant growth obscures the exposures. Cementation and grain features are easy to study here. Large, well-rounded and well-sorted 'millet seed' quartz grains can be seen with a hand-lens. Each has a thin **hematite** coating, giving it a red–brown colour.

In the upper quarry, as at the next two locations, sandstones are hard and particularly well-cemented with secondary silica. This

Figure 16.2 Dune cross-bedding in the Penrith Sandstone. *Photo*: J. Cockersole

Figure 16.3 Erosion plane in dune bedded Penrith Sandstone, Armathwaite (Location 5). *Photo*: E. Skipsey

occurs as **euhedral** crystalline overgrowths around the grains which sparkle when crystal facets reflect the light. The rock in the lower quarry is poorly cemented and grains can be readily separated by crushing between the fingers. Quartz veining, which occurs sporadically in the Penrith Sandstone, can be seen in the lower quarry.

Proceed to the group of old quarries in the Penrith Sandstone near Bowscar, by following the Bowscar–Lazonby road from the roundabout on the A6 (504339), 3 km north of Penrith, to the crest of the sandstone escarpment. Go through the gate on the south side of the road by the covered reservoir.

Location 2 (519345) is the working quarry of Bowscar. Please seek permission to visit from the quarry operator, Norwest Quarry Services (Tel: 0831–837943).

East–west faces of the quarry show the large-scale cross-bedding of the dune facies. A north–south face displays the very large-scale **trough cross-bedding** of the crescentic lee-slope of a dune. One floor of the quarry has been worked down to a bounding surface exposing joint systems running in two different sets of directions.

Return to the road and continue eastwards for about 1 km to the T-junction with the main Penrith to Lazonby road (532347). Turn left towards Lazonby. After about 500 m look out for a quarry entrance on the left with a Realstone Ltd sign.

Location 3 (533353) is the Realstone Quarry in the Penrith Sandstone. Permission must be sought from the Quarry Manager, Mr Dixon (Tel: 0768–68511), before visiting the site. The directions of dips of foreset beds and the axis of the large-scale trough bedding give clear indications of the dune form. It appears that stone is being extracted from a single dune.

Drive on to Lazonby, continue through the village and cross the river at Eden Bridge (551404). In Kirkoswald village turn right along the Glassonby road. After 1.5 km there is a small car park at Daleraven Bridge (565396). Follow the footpath, signposted 'Lacy's Caves', south along the river bank for about 1 km.

Location 4 (564383) is Lacy's Caves, excavated in about 1790 for the local landowner, Lt.-Col. Samuel Lacy. The caves are situated in a bluff of the poorly cemented aeolian Penrith Sandstone high above the east bank of the River Eden. Quartz veining is particularly well-developed here, the veins standing proud of the sandstone, showing that about 5 cm erosion of the rock has taken place since the caves were excavated.

Now drive to the northwest for about 6 km to the bridge across the River Eden at Armathwaite (507460). The Fox and Pheasant Hotel is on the east bank, 100 m or so from the bridge. Park your vehicle below this hotel and take the footpath leading south beside it. Turn right at the stile marking the Forestry Commission boundary and walk down through the woods to the riverside.

Location 5 (505452), Coombe Clints, is another sandstone bluff on the east bank of the River Eden. Rock faces run parallel to and at right angles to the **palaeo**wind direction and show the dune stratification in three dimensions. When river levels are low – all too rarely the case – an unusual exposure of dune bedding can be seen on a horizontal surface at the foot of the cliff. Look for the Tertiary Armathwaite **dyke** of dark **dolerite** which forms the natural weir (503453).

Recross the River Eden and turn right in Armathwaite village, following a narrow winding road north for 2.5 km. Turn right along a narrow lane (510486). After 500 m park at an access point by the river bank (514485). Follow the riverside footpath northwards for about 1 km along riverside cliffs.

Location 6 (514490) is this cliff area 3 km north of Armathwaite on the west bank of the River Eden. The cliffs consist of sequences of the brockram facies, already described and so very different from the dune sandstone. Mud flakes, fragments of **lithified**, chocolate-brown mud, show that shallow water was evaporating here during the Permo-Trias.

Excursion 2

This begins at Appleby. Park by the old Bongate Church (688199) and walk down the lane by the churchyard. Enter the river meadows through the first gate on the right.

Location 7 (687199) is Bongate Scar, an extensive old quarry face next to the river terrace. This shows large-scale dune stratification with cross-bedding and bounding surfaces in friable uncemented sandstone. In the far corner siltstone and clay galls (dry, curled 'clay-shavings', resulting from mud drying and cracking, then being embedded in a sand layer) suggest a minor episode of the sort of conditions that gave rise to the brockram facies.

Leave Appleby via the B6260, the Appleby to Orton road, and travel about 3 km south to the next location. Parking by the roadside

Figure 16.4 Fining-up sequences in the Brockram facies, Hoff Quarry (Location 8). *Photo*: E. Skipsey

(677180) is very limited, so be prepared to continue another 0.5 km to park by the New Inn in Hoff village and walk back.

Location 8 (676180), Hoff Quarry, a classic exposure of the brockram facies, is just off the B6260 Appleby–Orton road to the west near Burrells. Twenty metres of roughly bedded breccias are visible in many fining-up sequences (see Figure 16.4). **Imbrication** in pebbly layers and cross-bedding in sandy layers show the palaeo-flow directions. Most **clasts** are Carboniferous limestones, probably from the basin margins to the south, which were newly uplifted in Permian times.

Return to Appleby and leave along the B6542 to the southeast. Cross the A66, follow the signs for Hilton and Murton and take the partly fenced minor road on the left (711189) which leads across Appleby Golf Course. After 500 m park the vehicle on the wide right-hand verge. Walk 500 m along a footpath southeastwards, following the beck upstream, along an obvious glacial channel.

Location 9 (718188), George Gill, is an excellent exposure of aeolian sandstones. Large-scale dune cross-bedding is exposed on both sides of the channel, and recent wind action has emphasized the extensive quartz veining of the sandstone. Fluvial (brockram) incursions can be seen at the nearer edge of this exposure. Look for scour and fill (narrow pebble-filled channels) and clay galls.

Join the A66 and follow it to Brough, where you turn south on to the Kirkby Stephen road, the A685. Continue for about 2 km to the new bridge over the River Belah. Park in the layby on the left, part of the old road and bridge (793121). Pass through a stile at the south end of the old bridge and walk east.

Location 10 (795121) is Belah Scar, another classic section of the brockram facies, on the cliffs of the River Belah. There are several cycles of fluvial sandstones with basal scours filled with pebbles and gravels alongside the breccia-filled channels. The cycles fine-up through sands and silts to thin mud layers. Local thicker lenses of red mudstone suggest that flood waters were ponded in temporary lakes. The sandstone is generally horizontally bedded or structureless, but occasional layers of well-rounded, well-sorted sand with steep cross-bedding suggest temporary dune encroachment.

17 · Palaeozoic rocks of the Cross Fell district

Eric Skipsey *formerly of the Open University*

PURPOSE

To examine the Ordovician and Silurian rocks of the Cross Fell **inlier**, the Lower Carboniferous sediments and the Whin **Sill** of the Pennine scarp, mining remains in Great Rundale, Triassic sediments around Dufton, and **glacifluvial** features.

PRACTICAL DETAILS

One day with two optional excursions to other locations. Start from the public car park with toilets, in Dufton village, 5 km north of Appleby. There is a 10 km walk along footpaths and bridleways, including part of the Pennine Way. Access is restricted so keep to recognized footpaths. The route climbs 500 m to the Pennine escarpment and is *not recommended in bad weather*. Suitable strong footwear and appropriate clothing are essential. The sketch map (Figure 17.1) shows the locations visited.

OS MAPS: 1:25 000 Sheets NY 62 (Appleby) and NY 72 (Murton Fell)
1:50 000 Sheet 91

BGS MAP: 1:25 000 Geological Special Sheet – Cross Fell Inlier (together with Burgess, I. C. and Wadge, A. J. (1974), *The Geology of Cross Fell, Explanation of the Geological Special Sheet*, HMSO, London)

GEOLOGICAL SETTING

This excursion visits an area 6 km south of Cross Fell and covers part of the Pennine escarpment with the lower ground to the west. The

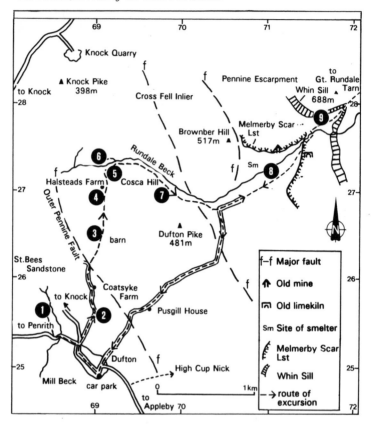

Figure 17.1 The Dufton Pike district.

scarp is formed of almost horizontal Lower Carboniferous sediments into which the late Carboniferous Whin Sill **dolerite** was intruded.

Varied Lower Palaeozoic rocks (400–500 **Ma** old) outcrop in the Cross Fell inlier at the foot of the scarp and form a 'window' revealing the basement of the Pennines. These older rocks, exposed in the Lake District fells, are believed to underlie the whole region at depth. The inlier is 1–3 km wide and stretches 25 km from Melmerby to Roman Fell. These Lower Palaeozoic rocks occur in large fault blocks with the major fault lines scoured by glacial erosion into deep valleys. Harder rocks of this age form the 'pikes', prominent conical hills between Knock and Murton. Table 17.1 shows how these rocks are correlated with the Lake District formations.

The lower ground to the west is underlain by drift-covered Triassic sediments, part of the Permo-Triassic sequences of the Vale of Eden and the source of the warm red sandstone used in buildings in fellside villages like Dufton.

The short steep dry valleys incised into the scarp face are glacial **meltwater channels**. These, and the extensive glacifluvial deposits, formed during the waning phase of the last glaciation.

Mining was widespread in the nineteenth century along the Pennine scarp. Lead mining ended in Great Rundale in 1898, and **barite** mining in 1924, though old lead spoil heaps were reworked for barite more recently. The old levels still open are very dangerous. *Do not enter without expert guidance.*

EXCURSION DETAILS

Location 1 (685254) is Millbeck Bridge Quarry, Dufton. Walk across the village green to the road junction north of the village and make a short diversion along the Penrith road. Alternatively the bridge may be reached through Dufton Woods along the path to 'The Ghyll'. Cross the bridge and take the footpath signposted 'St Cuthbert's

Period and Age	Dufton Sequence	Lake District Equivalent
	Sediments	
Triassic 220 Ma	St Bees Sandstone	St Bees Sandstone
—————— u n	c o n f o r m i t y ——————	
Lower Carboniferous (345–320 Ma)	Upper Alston Group (incl.) – Brig Hazle Sandst. – Tynebottom Lst Lower Limestone Group (incl.) – Melmerby Scar Lst Orton Group	Chief Limestone Group
—————— u n	c o n f o r m i t y ——————	
Ordovician (500–400 Ma)	Dufton Shales Knock Pike Tuff Formation Murton Formation	Dent Subgroup B.V.G. Skiddaw Group
	Intrusions	
Late Carboniferous Early Devonian	Whin Sill Dufton Microgranite	— Shap Granite

Table 17.1 The sequence of rocks seen in the Dufton Pike district and their Lake District equivalents.

Church'. In 100 m you reach an old quarry in St Bees Sandstone, which shows **cross-bedded** fine sandstones in 30–60 cm thick units with silty partings, brick red to yellow in colour.

Location 2 is Hurning Lane (689254). Return to the road junction and join the bridlepath, Hurning Lane, signposted 'Pennine Way' and running north towards Coatsyke Farm. A gateway on the right, 200 m along the lane, is a good viewpoint. The prominent break of slope beyond flat, drift-covered St Bees Sandstone marks the line of the Outer Pennine Fault. Lower Palaeozoic rocks of the Cross Fell inlier form the rugged Dufton Pike, and Carboniferous rocks the Pennine scarp beyond.

Location 3 (691266) is the sunken lane beyond Coatsyke Farm. After passing Coatsyke Farm the bridlepath eventually turns left. Follow the path waymarked by arrows along the sunken track. Excavation of a drainage ditch beside this track has exposed Lower Palaeozoic rocks of Silurian age. These are grey calcareous siltstones and mudstones of the Dufton Shales, correlated with the Dent Subgroup (formerly termed the Coniston Limestone Group) of the Lake District. Although poorly fossiliferous, fragments of brachiopods, trilobites and grapto-lites have been found.

Location 4 (691268) is a stone wall 250 m beyond Location 3. This wall is built of distinctive red blocks of red **porphyritic** *microgranite, with* **phenocrysts** of pink **feldspar**, rounded quartz and **muscovite** plates. They are from the nearby outcrop of Dufton Microgranite on the flanks of Dufton Pike. Several dykes of acid **porphyry**, of which this is the largest, outcrop in the north of the inlier. They appear to be early Devonian intrusions associated with granites like that at Shap.

Location 5 (691273) is Cosca Hill. Follow the track past the disused Hallsteads Farm over Cosca Hill, noticing the sand and gravel mounds on the hillside. These mounds are common on the north sides of spurs running down from the escarpment and are apparently related to sub-glacial drainage systems. They were probably depo-sited as bed-loads of sub-glacial streams and left standing as ridges when the ice melted. Glacial drainage channels, often now with little or no water, are common along the lower slopes of the Pennines. They are believed to have been formed by sub-glacial meltwater flow near the end of the last glaciation. You will see many such examples during this excursion.

Location 6 (692273) is Rundale Beck. A brief diversion takes you across an old clapperbridge over Rundale Beck, turning left through a gap stile and down along the north bank of the beck for 100–200 m. Look at the several large boulders on the floor of this deep valley. These are **erratic** blocks of the very distinctive Shap granite, identified by its large pink feldspar phenocrysts. During the Devensian (final) phase of the Ice Age, Lake District ice streamed east until checked by the Pennine escarpment. The distribution of these Shap granite boulders shows the directions of ice-flow. The main direction was southeast over Stainmore into the Tees valley and north Yorkshire. Another ice stream, which deposited these boulders, flowed northwards, crossing the Pennines north of Hartside into the Tyne valley.

Location 7 (698271–700269) is the northern flank of Dufton Pike. Return across the clapperbridge and follow the path up Great Rundale towards the escarpment. Beyond the second stile sheep scrapes in the scree expose the Borrowdale Volcanic Group rocks of Dufton Pike. These are mainly **rhyolitic ash-flow tuffs** or **ignimbrites**, compact and fine-grained, appearing streaky in hand specimen and weathering to pale shades.

Location 8 (710271), Pack Mule Mine road, is reached by the path which eventually joins the road to the Dufton Fell mines near a sheep pen. Walk towards the escarpment until you reach a gate beyond which there are excellent views. The cone-shaped Dufton Pike is behind you, with the Eden Valley beyond, and the eastern Lake District fells form the skyline. The crags of Melmerby Scar Limestone 'vee' deep into the valley head of Great Rundale with screes of Orton Group rocks and the Basement Bed sandstones tumbling down to the valley floor (see the photograph, Figure 17.2). Brownber Hill to the north, beyond a fault line, consists of siltstones of the Murton Formation, with white quartz veins glistening in the steeply dipping beds.

Traces of mining can still be found. An **adit** entrance is visible at the base of the limestone across the valley, as is the line of a long flue climbing the hillside from a demolished smelt house. Follow the track up the valley and look at the Melmerby Scar Limestone. This is a pale grey to buff bioclastic limestone, around 35 m thick. An old limekiln makes a good lunch stop.

Figure 17.2 The Melmerby Scar Limestone outcrop in Great Rundale.
Photo: E. Skipsey

Location 9 (ca 717277) is the Dufton Fell Mines, an extensive series of levels at the head of Great Rundale where **galena** was extracted from several east-west trending veins. Although lead mining ceased in 1898 the old spoil heaps have been reworked for barite. Evidence of this reworking is still obvious, particularly in the upper reaches of the valley where large areas of black shale have been disturbed. Many blocks with barite, **ankerite, dolomite** and patches of galena can be found.

The higher parts of the scarp consist of thin limestones, mudstones and sandstone horizons of Lower Carboniferous age. Immediately below the Tynebottom Limestone is the dark-coloured Whin Sill with its vertical **jointing**, so different to the bedding of the sediments.

The country changes dramatically at the top of the escarpment to typical Pennine moorland with peat bogs. The massive fine-grained sandstone now being worked in a small quarry beside the track is the Low Brig Hazle. This and the more extensive High Brig Hazle form the sandstone cap to the Pennine escarpment. Not far from the track is Great Rundale Tarn, the source of Maize Beck which flows east to join the River Tees.

Return to Dufton along the mine road past Pusgill House.

Optional Extensions

Knock Pike Quarry (687285) worked for roadstone, has the most extensive local exposure of Borrowdale Volcanic Group rocks. Take the road to Milburn Grange from Knock village, turning right after 400 m along a minor road running northeast towards Great Dun Fell. After another 2 km a track leads to the large quarry behind Knock Pike. *Wear your safety helmet and keep clear of the dangerous quarry walls.*

Part of a thick ash-flow unit is exposed. The pale green, fine-grained rock has a strongly developed streaky **eutaxitic** texture, due to the intense compaction of included pumice fragments.

High Cup Nick (745262) visible from many parts of the Vale of Eden, is one of the best-known geological features of Northern England. The return trip to the top of High Cup Nick and Maize Beck is a strenuous walk of 14 km, which requires a full day. Follow the Pennine Way southeast from Dufton village past Bow Hall and Peeping Hill.

The western edge of the quartz-dolerite Whin Sill which underlies the whole of Northeast England outcrops along the Pennine scarp. It reaches its maximum thickness of 30 m at the head of High Cup Nick where it appears in the strata underlying the Tynebottom Limestone. It forms a conspicuous line of crags, with characteristic columnar jointing, around the head of this spectacular valley. The top surface of the sill, with its chilled margin, is well exposed to the east.

Redbanks Quarry, Dufton Ghyll (695245), is the best exposure of St Bees Sandstone in the Eden Valley. It is a fine-grained chocolate red sandstone with flakes of shiny mica on the bedding planes. This is a well laminated rock with nearly horizontal bedding unlike the steep dips of the cross bedding in the Penrith Sandstone. The St Bees Sandstone was an important local building stone, this quarry providing stone for Dufton and neighbouring villages.

18 · The Lower Carboniferous rocks of West Edenside

Alan Day *formerly Field Secretary, Westmorland Geological Society*

PURPOSE

To examine **cyclothems** in the Brigantian stage of the Lower Carboniferous.

PRACTICAL DETAILS

An easy half-day's excursion. Orton village (622083), which is approached from Junction 38 on the M6, is our starting point. It has a pub, small shops, and public toilets. Walking distances are quite short to old quarries and open ground near the roadside. Appropriate, windproof clothing and suitable, strong footwear are recommended. There are no restrictions on access. A vehicle is essential as the locations are widely spaced. There is adequate parking for cars at or near the roadside, but the roads followed are unsuitable for coaches.

OS MAP: 1:50 000 Sheet 91

GEOLOGICAL SETTING

This excursion continues up the Lower Carboniferous succession north of the last location visited during Excursion 1 in this book. Dips are usually gentle, to the northeast, and rocks 'young' northwards into the Eden valley. The Brigantian rocks overlie the Asbian, and consist of a series of cyclothems. The general sequence within the cyclothems is (from bottom to top) limestone–shale–sandstone–coal (the latter only present occasionally). Individual cyclothems differ in matters of detail from this broad pattern.

The cyclothems are interpreted as sediments laid down during either fluctuating sea levels or periodic subsidence of a basin. The

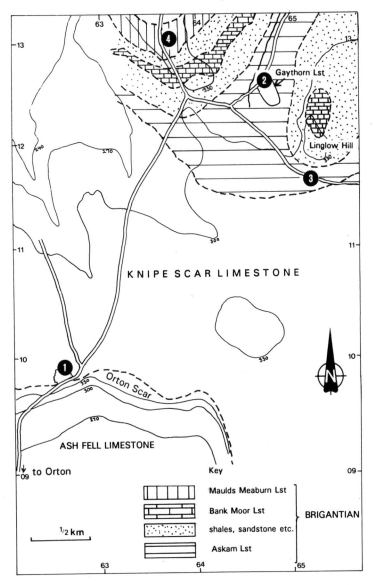

Figure 18.1 A simplified geological map of the Carboniferous Limestone of West Edenside.

limestones are marine deposits, with the shales being partly marine and partly deltaic. The sandstones were laid down in more varied conditions, ranging from river channels with overbank deposition, through deltaic environments, to coastal bays.

The scenery has been modified by glacial action. Patchy drift drapes the landscape and **meltwater channels** have been cut into solid rock.

Figure 18.1 is a simplified geological map of the area, showing the locations visited.

EXCURSION DETAILS

Leave Orton on the B6260 going northwards towards Appleby. Continue to the summit of Orton Scar and pull into the old quarry to the left of the road.

Location 1 (627098) is this quarry, where Knipe Scar Limestone of the Asbian Stage is exposed, with heather-clad, sandy soils above. This stop allows comparison with the overlying Brigantian rocks seen later. The Knipe Scar Limestone here is light grey and poorly bedded. If you break open a loose fragment you should see irregular light and dark grey patches, thought to be due to **bioturbation** by organisms that lived in the sediment. Fossils are not common, but notice the large curved sections of the brachiopod *Gigantoproductus* and the occasional transverse sections of solitary and colonial corals.

Continue northwards down the dip slope of the Knipe Scar Limestone for about 3 km. Turn right along the unfenced minor road

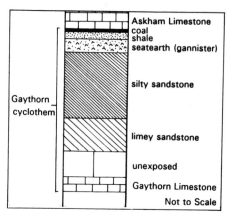

Figure 18.2 The rocks of the Gaythorn cyclothem.

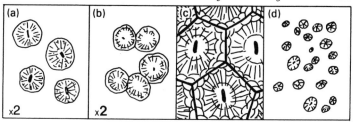

Figure 18.3 Fossils of the Carboniferous Limestone: (a) *Siphonodendron pauciradiale*; (b) *Diphyphylloid sp.*; (c) *Actinocyathus (Lonsdaleia) floriformis*; (d) *Siphonodendron junceum.*

signposted 'Great Asby'. After about 300–400 m take the narrow road to the left, descend the hill for about 500 m and park on the grass by the cattle grid with the head of Scale Beck to your right.

Location 2 (647127) is this parking place. Walk upstream a short distance and notice that Scale Beck is actively depositing **tufa**. The dark-coloured well-bedded rock in the stream bed is the basal (Gaythorn) limestone of a thin cyclothem. Continue upstream into a small gully where a limy sandstone appears, followed by a thick grey sandstone behind the small waterfall. Next in the succession is a knobbly bed of sandstone with many rootlets penetrating it. This is a **ganister**. A thin shale and even thinner coal follow to complete the succession. Figure 18.2 illustrates this, the Gaythorn cyclothem, which has no shale immediately above the basal limestone.

The next rock type is a thick limestone (the Askham Limestone), the start of the Askham cyclothem. This also is a dark limestone and fossils can be found very easily in the broken rocks on the gully floor. These will probably include the corals *Siphonodendron pauciradiale* (Figure 18.3a), *Diphyphylloid sp.* (Figure 18.3b) and brachiopods such as *Spirifer* and *Gigantoproductus*.

Return to the Great Asby road and turn sharp left (southeast). Continue up the hill to the cattle grid named on the 1:50 000 map.

Location 3 (651118) is the parking area on the grass verge by this cattle grid. Walk uphill, following the wall that leads to the top of Linglow Hill to the northeast. Changes in vegetation types and in the composition of this wall indicate changes in the underlying rock types. Between the roadside and a break of slope the vivid green grass with a few incipient sink holes (better developed east of the wall) marks the outcrop of the Askham Limestone. Above the break of slope are rank, duller grasses, and occasional layers of shale crop out. Near the hilltop, heather grows around sandstone exposures. This is a continuation of the Askham cyclothem with the shale and sandstone at its top being exposed. This, the younger Askham cyclothem, is much thicker than the underlying Gaythorn one.

Return to the B6260 and drive northwards (over the Bank Moor cyclothem) as far as a quarry on the right. North of here, you will find safe and convenient roadside parking.

Location 4 (637130) is this rather messy quarry. Its richly fossiliferous limestone is the basal unit of the Maulds Meaburn cyclothem. *Please do not hammer the rock face*, as loose material on the quarry floor contains many fossils. Notice the even bedding of this impure limestone. The following coral species have been recorded in this quarry: *Diphyphyllum sp, Actinocyathus (Lonsdaleia) floriformis* (Figure 18.3c); *Lithostrotion sp,* (Figure 1.4c) *Siphonodendron junceum* (Figure 18.3d); *Dibunophyllum bipartum* (Figure 1.4d); and *Palaeosmilia murchisoni* (Figure 1.4e).

Glossary

acritarch A marine microfossil, used in dating Lower Palaeozoic rocks.

adit Horizontal or gently sloping mine entrance.

air fall tuff See **tuff**.

alabaster A fine-grained, massive variety of **gypsum**.

alluvial fan A gently sloping half-cone of material deposited by a stream where its gradient suddenly decreases.

amphiboles A group of ferromagnesian silicate minerals found in igneous and metamorphic rocks. **Hornblende** is the most common.

amygdales Almond-shaped cavities (originally gas bubbles) in lava, filled with later-formed minerals such as quartz, calcite or **chlorite**.

andalusite An aluminium silicate, formed during low-grade **thermal metamorphism** of shales or mudstones. Crystals are elongated and prismatic, known as **chiastolite** if they contain dark cross-shaped inclusions.

andesite A fine-grained igneous rock composed of calcium feldspars, quartz and pyroxene, dark grey, green or black, sometimes with **phenocrysts** of white **feldspar**, **biotite**, **hornblende** or **augite**.

anhydrite An **evaporite**, an anhydrous form of calcium sulphate, colourless, white or tinted. Harder than **gypsum**.

ankerite A pale-coloured, complex iron carbonate.

aplite A light-coloured, fine-grained, igneous rock penetrating granite in thin veins, probably formed in the final stages of crystallization of a magma.

arête A knife-edge ridge, eaten into by **corries**.

ash flow tuff See **tuff**.

augite See **pyroxene**.

aureole The area around an intrusion, affected by **thermal metamorphism**. See **metamorphism**.

axial-plane cleavage See **cleavage**.

azurite A deep azure-blue copper carbonate, often associated with **malachite**.

barite Barium sulphate, white, colourless or tinted, dense, brittle mineral, often with flat crystal faces.

basalt   A common, fine-grained, usually dark-coloured volcanic lava, with calcium **feldspars** and **pyroxenes** but no quartz.

batholith   A large, granitic intrusion associated with an **orogenic** belt. Its upper surfaces can crop out. Its heat metamorphosed the rocks it intruded.

biotite   A brown, black or dark-green **mica**.

bioturbation   The disturbance of sediments by animal activity, e.g. by crustaceans' feeding burrows.

braided   A type of stream, transporting coarse particles, with many wide, shallow, frequently changing channels. Often choked by its own debris.

breccia   A poorly sorted deposit with large angular fragments set in a fine matrix.

Brockram   The Permo-Triassic **breccia** of the Vale of Eden and West Cumbria.

bryozoa   Small, branching, colonial, marine animals.

Caledonian   A mountain-building episode (**orogeny**) in late Silurian and Devonian times, caused by a collision of continents across northern Britain and Scandinavia.

cerussite   Lead carbonate, a very dense white to grey mineral.

chalcopyrite   Copper pyrites, a brassy yellow mineral with iridescent tarnish, softer than iron **pyrites** which it resembles.

chiastolite   See **andalusite**.

chlorite   A group of green, complex silicates formed by the alteration of minerals such as **hornblende** and **biotite**. The cause of the green tinge of many BVG rocks.

clast   A fragment of pre-existing rock incorporated in a sediment, e.g. a pebble in a conglomerate.

cleavage   Planes formed from compressive forces along which rocks split, usually parallel to fold axes (**axial-plane cleavage**) and independent of bedding.

clints   Flat-topped surfaces, following bedding planes, between **grykes** in a limestone pavement.

conglomerate   A sedimentary rock with large well-rounded fragments such as pebbles, set in a fine matrix. Usually water deposited.

convolute bedding   A sedimentary structure formed while the sediment was unconsolidated. It is distinguished from folding by being confined to individual beds.

cordierite   A complex mineral formed during the **thermal metamorphism** of fine-grained rocks. Forms small black spots in the **hornfels** of the Skiddaw Granite **aureole**.

corrie   A glacially eroded basin, at the head of a pre-existing valley, with a steep head wall and steep sides enclosing an armchair-shaped hollow.

crag and tail   The crag is a glacially eroded, resistant rock outcrop facing up-valley; the tail, often of weaker material, is on its down-valley side.

cross-bedding (lamination)   Inclined laminae or bedding surfaces, differing from the general dip of the bed and indicating direction of current flow.

cyclothem   A repeated sequence or cycle of sediments, common in the Carboniferous.

dacite   A lava with a composition between **andesite** and **rhyolite**.

dip fault   See **fault**.

disconformity   See **unconformity**.

dolerite   A medium-grained igneous rock, black or dark green on un-weathered surfaces. Chemically the equivalent of basalt.

dolomite   A white, yellow or brown mineral, a carbonate of calcium and magnesium, often replacing calcite in limestones. The name is also used for a rock composed of this mineral.

drumlin   A streamlined, 'whale-backed' low hill of boulder clay, usually occurring in swarms parallel to the direction of ice flow, with the blunt, steeper end pointing 'up-glacier'.

dyke   A narrow, wall-like intrusion cutting across the bedding of the host rock.

enclave   An area of older rock included within an igneous intrusion.

epidote   A pale, yellowish-green, silicate mineral, common in BVG rocks, formed by either low-grade **regional metamorphism** or **metasomatism**.

erratic   A rock transported by ice from its original source.

esker   A long, narrow, winding, steep-sided, low ridge of **glacifluvial** sand and gravel.

euhedral   A fully developed crystal form.

eutaxitic   An **ignimbrite** texture with dark streaks (**fiamme**) in a white-weathering, fine-grained matrix.

evaporite   A mineral precipitated by the evaporation of saline water, the most common examples being halite, **gypsum**, **anhydrite** and **dolomite**.

facies   The features of a rock indicating the environment in which it formed.

fault   Fracture in rock along which there has been displacement. A **dip** or **normal fault** runs parallel to the dip of the rocks, with mainly vertical movements; a **strike-slip** (**wrench**, or **tear**) fault shows a mainly horizontal movement parallel to the strike of the fault plane; a **thrust** is a low-angle fault in which older rocks have overridden younger; **fault gouge** is fine material produced by the grinding together of rocks on either side of a fault.

feldspars   The main group of rock-forming minerals occurring in almost all igneous rocks, often as rectangular crystals. Differences in magma composition and crystallization give rise to different feldspars. The most important are pink **orthoclase**, a potassium feldspar; and the white **plagioclase** series of sodium and calcium feldspars.

fiamme   Elongated, dark, streaky, flattened pumice fragments found in welded **ignimbrites**.

flame structure   Small tongues of fine-grained sediment pushed up into overlying coarser materials.

flow-banding The alignment of crystals due to differential movement in a lava flow.

fluorite (fluorspar) Calcium fluoride, a colourless, white, blue, purple or yellow mineral, which may have cubic or octahedral crystals.

flute cast (mark) A groove cut into mud by a fast-flowing current and later filled with coarser sediment.

foraminiferid A small, single-celled marine animal.

fragipan (fragic) A dense, brittle, compact horizon deep in an acidic soil profile.

gabbro A coarse-grained igneous rock, chemically similar to basalt, consisting essentially of **plagioclase** and **augite**.

galena Lead sulphide, the main ore of lead.

gangue The unwanted minerals in an orebody.

ganister (gannister) A fine sandstone **seat-earth** containing root-traces and underlying a coal seam. Almost pure silica.

garnet A complex silicate, forming very hard, rounded crystals, usually brown or red in colour and commonly found in metamorphic rocks.

glacifluvial Referring to bedded sand and gravel deposited by meltwater streams associated with glaciers.

graded bedding A sedimentary texture in which the grain size decreases up from the base of a bed, resulting from the settling of material in a waning current.

granodiorite A coarse-grained, often pale-coloured, igneous rock, containing quartz, **plagioclase** and sodium feldspars with some **biotite**. The most common type of 'granite', found in batholiths.

granophyre A fine-grained, often pale pink igneous rock, similar in composition to granite, with intergrowing quartz and feldspar crystals, sometimes forming **phenocrysts**.

gravity anomaly An unusual gravity value. Negative (lower than expected) anomalies are found over hidden granitic intrusions.

greisen A coarse-grained pale rock, consisting of mica and quartz, formed by the alteration of crystalline granite by fluorine-rich hot fluids which broke down feldspars in the final stages of crystallization.

greywacke A poorly sorted sandstone with angular rock fragments and much clay, often deposited by **turbidity** currents.

ground moraine See **moraine**.

grykes Vertical clefts in limestone pavement, up to 1 m deep, formed by solution of limestone along joints.

gypsum An **evaporite**, calcium sulphate. Usually colourless or white, it is easily scratched by a fingernail.

hanging valley A tributary valley high above the floor of the main glacial trough.

hematite An iron oxide ore mineral, steel grey to black in colour. It may form rounded masses (**kidney** ore) or shiny, blade-like crystals (**specularite**).

Hercynian A mountain-building episode (**orogeny**) at the end of the Carboniferous Period, which mainly affected southwestern Britain and northwestern France.

hornblende A dark greenish **amphibole**, sometimes with elongated crystals, common in igneous and metamorphic rocks.

hornfels A fine-grained, flinty, hard rock produced by intense **thermal metamorphism** near an intrusion.

hydrothermal Term used to describe the high-temperature mineralized fluids associated with igneous activity.

Iapetus An ocean which separated the Lake District/England from Scotland/North America before its closure by continental drift at the end of the Silurian Period.

ignimbrite A pumice-rich **pyroclastic** rock, formed by a volcanic ash flow in which temperatures were hot enough to weld fragments together, producing **fiamme** and **eutaxitic** textures.

imbricate A texture in **breccias** and **conglomerates** where the long axes of pebbles lean down the direction of current flow.

inlier An isolated area of older rocks surrounded by younger.

interstadial A short phase of warmer climate during a glacial period.

joints Cracks in a rock along which there has been no displacement. Joints may be due to shrinkage, release of pressure or the flexing of folds. Those at the crest of folds are known as **tension gashes**.

kame A steep-sided ridge or conical hill of bedded **glacifluvial** material.

kaolinite China clay, formed by the breakdown of **feldspars**, either by chemical weathering or by **hydrothermal** action.

karst Limestone scenery, with features such as caves, dry valleys and limestone pavements.

kettle hole A depression in glacial drift (which may contain a small lake) formed where a stagnant ice mass melted.

kidney ore See **hematite**.

laminae Layers of sedimentary rock under 1 cm thick.

lateral moraine See **moraine**.

lapilli Volcanic ash fragments up to the size of peanuts (60 mm).

lithic fragments Dense or crystalline fragments within a **pyroclastic** flow.

lithification The processes whereby unconsolidated sediments are converted to rock.

lithology The general character of a rock.

load cast A bulbous feature on the base of a sandstone bed, formed when the sand was pressed down into an underlying mud before lithification.

Ma Symbol for million years.

malachite A bright green copper carbonate, often occurring as an encrustation and sometimes found with **azurite**.

marker band (bed) A thin, distinctive bed which can be recognized over a wide area. It can be used as a time marker and to correlate rocks.

megacryst A large well-formed crystal set in a fine groundmass.

meltwater channel A valley eroded by glacial meltwater and unrelated to present drainage.

metamorphism Changes in rock in the solid state caused by heat, pressure and chemically active fluids. **Thermal metamorphism** is due to heat flow from an igneous intrusion into surrounding rocks, creating an **aureole**, with new or realigned minerals. **Regional metamorphism** describes the large-scale changes due to heat and pressure, leading to the formation of new minerals, and **slaty cleavage** in fine-grained rocks.

metasomatism Metamorphic changes caused by chemically active fluids entering and migrating through a rock.

molybdenite A very soft silvery mineral, molybdenum sulphide.

moraine An accumulation of ill-sorted glacial **till** of varied origin. A **lateral moraine** accumulated at the side of a glacier; a **terminal moraine** is a curved ridge in front of active ice; a **recessional moraine** marks a pause in the retreat of a glacier or an ice sheet; and a **ground moraine** is a thick sheet of boulder clay dropped from the base of melting ice.

muscovite A transparent, pale-coloured, flexible mineral; a form of mica.

oligoclase A variety of **plagioclase feldspar**.

oolite A limestone composed of spherical sand-size grains.

orogeny A mountain-building period, taking place over tens of millions of years and culminating in a continent–continent collision.

orthoclase The most common potassium **feldspar**, often pink in colour.

outlier An isolated area of younger rocks surrounded by older rocks.

palaeo A prefix, meaning very old.

periglacial Describing the area adjacent to an ice sheet or glacier, with permanently frozen ground just below the surface and very active freeze–thaw processes.

perthitic A texture formed by intergrowth of sodium and potassium **feldspars**.

phenocryst A large, well-formed crystal set in a finer groundmass. This igneous texture is called **porphyritic**.

picrite An ultrabasic rock consisting mainly of ferromagnesian minerals.

plagioclase A family of sodium and calcium **feldspars**, often with white, rectangular crystals. See **feldspars**.

plug Any small, more or less vertical intrusion.

pluton A deep-seated igneous intrusion.

point bar A deposit on the inside of a river bend or meander.

porphyritic See **phenocryst**.

porphyroblast A relatively large crystal which grew in a finer-grained groundmass during metamorphism.

porphyry An igneous rock containing large crystals set in a fine ground-mass.

prod marks Small asymmetrical impact marks of objects dragged over a soft, muddy surface, now usually filled with a cast.

pyrite pale yellow, hard iron sulphide, often displaying cubic crystals.

pyroclastic Describing volcanic rocks consisting of broken particles.

pyroclastic surge and **fall** See **tuff**.

pyromorphite A very dense, green, brown or yellow lead mineral.

pyroxene A family of ferromagnesian minerals common in igneous rocks. **Augite**, with its greenish-black crystals is the most common type.

pyrrhotite A coppery-bronze iron sulphide.

radiometric dating A method of dating certain rocks and minerals using the known rates of decay of radioactive elements.

recessional moraine See **moraine**.

rhyodacite A lava, usually **porphyritic**, with quartz and **plagioclase phenocrysts**.

rhyolite A fine-grained volcanic rock, similar in composition to granite, sometimes pale in colour consisting of quartz, **micas**, and **orthoclase** and sodium feldspars.

ripple drift (lamination or bedding) A sedimentary structure formed by currents during rapid deposition. See **trough cross-bedding**.

rip-up clast An eroded fragment of an underlying bed incorporated into the bed above.

roche moutonnée A glacial erosion feature; a rock mound with a gently sloping upstream side smoothed and scratched by the ice, and a steeper, craggy, ice-plucked downstream side.

rugose (coral) A type of Palaeozoic coral in which septa (vertical plates like the spokes of a wheel) are visible in cross-section.

seat earth A clay-rich, pale-coloured, fossil soil underlying a coal seam, often with root traces.

sericite A type of mica often found in **greisen**.

sill An intrusion running generally parallel to the bedding of the rock which it intruded.

slate A fine-grained rock altered by low-grade **regional metamorphism** to give closely spaced **cleavage**.

slickenside The polishing and grooving on a fault plane caused by the abrasive action of rock sliding against rock.

sole marks A general term for sedimentary structures on the base of beds. See **flute** and **load casts**.

solifluction Slow down-slope movement of masses of surface material saturated with water. Common on gentle slopes in **periglacial** conditions.

specularite   See **hematite**.

sphalerite (zinc blende)   Zinc sulphide, the main zinc ore; light to dark brown or black in colour.

stadial   A short period of increasing cold or advancing ice.

stope   Extraction of ore from above or below a tunnel in a mine.

strike-slip   See **fault**.

stylolites   Irregular sutures in some limestones, caused by pressure solution.

subduction   The process whereby an ocean plate is overridden by another plate and destroyed.

superimposed drainage   A system of drainage developed on a younger series of rocks now largely removed by erosion, which cuts across the structures of underlying older rocks.

tabular cross-bedding   A sedimentary structure caused by the migration down current of straight-crested asymmetric ripples or dunes.

tabulate (coral)   A type of palaeozoic colonial coral in which the most obvious features are horizontal transverse plates, the tabulae.

tear   See **fault**.

tension gash   See **joints**.

thrust   See **fault**.

till   A glacially deposited mass of ill-sorted rocks and clay. Also known as boulder clay.

topaz   A very hard, pale-coloured mineral found in granites and greisen.

tourmaline   A very hard silicate mineral, sometimes black, occurring in granites, and metamorphosed rocks.

trace fossil   Marks left in sediment by the activity of animals, e.g. footprints or burrows.

trough cross-bedding   A sedimentary structure caused by the migration down-current of asymmetric tongue-shaped ripples or dunes.

trough end   The very steep rock wall at the head of a deep glacial trough, above which there is usually a group of **corries**.

truncated spur   A valley-side spur, whose lower end has been cut off by glacial erosion and become much steeper.

tufa   Calcium carbonate deposit forming today from groundwater in limestone districts.

tuff   **Lithified** volcanic ash. **Air fall tuffs** are volcanic fragments falling to the ground after explosive eruptions; **pyroclastic surge** and **flow** (**ash flow**) deposits are due to volcanic blasts of ground-hugging, turbulent masses of gas and fluidized fragments. **Ignimbrites** are a product of such processes.

turbidite   A rock unit formed by the settling of material in water following the passage of a turbidity current. The latter is a slurry of mud, sand and water flowing down an underwater slope. The sedimentary units often show **graded bedding**.

twinning   The arrangement of a mineral's crystal lattice so that one part of the crystal is a mirror image of the other.

unconformity   A surface that separates two strata and which marks a time interval when there was no deposition. Often the rocks above and below the unconformity show differences in the direction and amount of dip etc. A **disconformity** is an **unconformity** without change in dip or strike.

vesicular texture (vesicles)   See **amygdales**.
volcaniclastic   A layered rock consisting of fragments of volcanic material.

wadi   A gorge-like, water-cut valley (without a permanent stream) in desert or semi-desert regions.
wrench   See **fault**.

zinc blende   See **sphalerite**.

Geological and Mineralogical Museum Collections in Cumbria

There are a number of good museums in Cumbria but all have relatively small geological sections. The main ones are listed below with information on their location and a telephone number for further information. If a special journey is planned, it is usually advisable to check on opening hours, particularly out of the tourist season. Museums with an entrance fee are marked with an asterisk:

CALDBECK: Mining Museum* (06998) 369 Specializes in mining operations, particularly in the Caldbeck Fells. Large collection of old photographs, mining tools and minerals.

CARLISLE: Tullie House Museum* (0228) 34761 A splendid museum mainly featuring local archaeology and history. Geological reference collection available by prior arrangement.

CONISTON: Ruskin Museum* (05394) 41387 Relating mainly to the life and works of John Ruskin but includes his small mineral collection.

KENDAL: Natural History and archaeology Museum* (0539) 721374 Covers the whole field of natural history including geology.

EGREMONT: The West Cumbria Mines Research Group Museum, Florence Mine. This museum specializes in West Cumbrian mining history and houses the Edgar Shackleton collection of rocks and fossils. Telephone Dave Banks **(0946) 823812** to arrange access.

KESWICK: Museum and Art Gallery* (07687) 73263 Closed in winter. A time capsule gem of a late Victorian museum including a small but useful collection of local rocks, fossils and minerals.

PENRITH: Museum (0768) 64671 A small collection on local geology, archaeology and history.

WHITEHAVEN: Museum (0946) 693111/67575 A small museum specializing in local history with mining memorabilia.

As Cumbria is a popular tourist area, there are a number of visitor centres which often have displays on local features including geology. They can also be useful sources of information:

BROCKHOLE National Park Centre* (09662) 6601 Between Ambleside and Windermere.

GRIZEDALE Forest Centre* (0229) 860 373 South of Hawkshead.

SEATOLLER Dalehead Base (07687) 77294 The head of Borrowdale, south of Keswick.

WHINLATTER Forest Centre (07687) 78469 West of Keswick.

Further Reading

General

Lynas, B. (1994) *Lakeland Rocky Rambles – Geology beneath your feet*, Sigma Books. (This uses 10 excursions to explain in considerable detail the geology of Lakeland).

Moseley, F. (ed) (1978) *The Geology of the Lake District*, Occasional Publication No. 3, Yorkshire Geological Society, Leeds.
(Although 13 years old, this is the most comprehensive volume describing the geology of the area, with 18 separate chapters written by experts.)

Moseley, F. (1990) *The Lake District*, The Geologists' Association Guide.
(This gives an up-to-date summary of current interpretations. It provides details of 25 new geological excursions to key sites in Cumbria where current geological problems and interpretations may be examined in the field. The level of much of the material is quite advanced.)

Shackleton, E. H. (1975) *Lakeland Geology* (Reprinted 1991), Dalesman, Clapham.
(This is the original introduction to Lake District geology that interested so many in the subject.)

Smith, R. A. (1974) *A Bibliography of the Geology and Geomorphology of Cumbria*, The Cumberland Geological Society, Workington.
Smith, R. A. (1990) *A Bibliography of the Geology and Geomorphology of Cumbria, Part 2 (1974–1990)*, The Cumberland Geological Society, Workington.
(These comprehensive lists of Lake District geological literature include nearly 2000 individual items and provide classified indexes under a wide range of headings.)

Specific

Adams, J. (1988) *Mines of the Lake District*, Dalesman, Clapham.
(This is a comprehensive description of the old mines, based on recent exploration and illustrated with many maps, diagrams and cross-sections.)

Boardman, J. (1988) *Classic Landforms of the Lake District*, Geographical Association Guide No. 8.
(Case studies of five classic areas of Lakeland.)

146

Cooper, M. P. and Stanley, C. J. (1990) *Minerals of the English Lake District, Caldbeck Fells*, Natural History Museum Publications.
(A very readable, finely illustrated description of mines in the Caldbeck Fells).

Cumbria Amenity Trust Mining History Society (1992) *Beneath the Lakeland Fells*, Red Earth Publications, Ulverston, Cumbria. (A general description of mining in Cumbria, particularly interesting about the organization and technology of the old mines. Many old photographs.)

Johnson, R. H. (ed) (1985) *The Geomorphology of North-West England*, Manchester University Press.
(Not exclusively our area, but with current ideas about the landforms and geomorphology of the Lake District.)

Macchi, L. (no date) *A Field Guide to the Continental Permo-Triassic Rocks of Cumbria and Northwest Cheshire*, the Liverpool Geological Society.
(An authoritative analysis).

Moseley, F. (1983) *The Volcanic Rocks of the Lake District*, Macmillan, London.
(An easy-to-read explanation of the volcanics with excursion guides to popular areas.)

Moseley, F. (1986) *Geology and Scenery in the Lake District*, Macmillan, London.
(A guide to 14 areas in the Lake District, explaining the relationship between geology and scenery.)

Petterson, M. G. (1990) Recent Developments Concerning the Borrowdale Volcanic Group in the English Lake District, *Proc. Cumberland Geol. Soc.*, 5, Part 2, 156–168.
(An excellent summary of recent thinking on the Borrowdale Volcanic Group.)

Skipsey, E. (1994) *Geological Excursions in the Eden Valley*. Cumbria RIGS Group, English Nature, Bowness on Windermere.
(A brief, user-friendly guide to the Permo-Triassic rocks of the Eden Valley).

Young, B (1987) *Glossary of the Minerals of the Lake District and Adjoining Areas*, British Geological Survey.
(A detailed reference work for the mineralogist.)

Index

Page numbers in **bold** refer to figures and tables.

air fall tuff, *see* tuff
alluvial fans 9–10, 71, 90, 117
Alpine 10
amphibole 22
andalusite 53, 102
andesite **2**, 5–7, 22, 24, 31, 52–3, 55–7, 68, 76
anhydrite 10, 63, 65
ankerite 105, 128
aplite 22, 24, 49
Appleby **x**, 115, 120–1, 123, 132
arête 71
Armathwaite **x**, 120
Armboth Dyke 7, 83–7
Asbian stage 16–18, 35–40, 130, 132
Ashfell Limestone 16–18, 131
Askham cyclothem 130–3
Aulophyllum 111, 114
Axophyllum 17–18

Bannisdale Formation 23, 38
barite 22, 76, 105, 125, 128
basalt 5, 56–8
Bassenthwaite 76–8, 96, 99–100
batholith 7–9, 46, 102
Beacon Edge 117
Belah Scar 122
biotite **2**, 44
bioturbation 111, 132
Birk Riggs Formation **28**, 32–3
Birkrigg Common 34–8
Borrowdale Volcanic Group (BVG) **x**, **2–3**, 5–8, 13, 20, 22, 26–33, 43–5, 46–53, 54–61, 66, 68, 69–74, 75–6, 83, 88, 99–100, 125, 129
boulder clay, *see* till
Bowder Stone 82
braided stream 15, 91
Brathay Formation 27–9, 32
breccia 10, 63, 115–17, 120–2
Brigantian stage 35–40, 111, 130–4
Brockram 10, 63, 66, 115–17, 120–2
Brotherswater 88–94
Brough 115, 122
Browgill Formation 29–32

Buttermere 4, 69–74
Buttermere Formation 70–4

calcite 22–3, 29, 38
Caldbeck 107–14
Caledonian 1, 4, 8–10, 42, 70, 84, 102
Caninia 40
Carboniferous Limestone **2–3**, 8–9, 13–18, 34–40, 66, 107–14, **116**, 121, **125**–9, 130–4
Carrock Fell Complex, 7, 103
Castle Crag 77, 79, 82
Castlehead **96**, 99–100
Caudale **89**, 91–4
Causey Pike Thrust 4–8
cerussite 76
Chaetetes 17
chalcopyrite 22, 105
chiastolite 102–4
chlorite 15, 58, 84
clast 14–15, 58, 66–7, 74, 121
cleavage 4, 8, 23, 28, 32, 43, 53, 70, 72, 86, 104
Clisiophyllum 40
coal 109, 130–2
Coal Measures **2–3**, 9, 63–5
Coldwell Formation 28, 33
conglomerate 8, 13–15, 74
Coniston Subgroup 23, 28, 32, 41, 43–5
contact metamorphism, *see* metamorphism, thermal
cordierite 102–4
corrie 11, 71, 74, 82, 90–4, 96
crag and tail 82, 98–9
cross-bedded 15, 32–3, 66, 116, 119–21, 126
Cross Fell 1, 5, 123–6
cross-stratification, *see* cross-bedded
Crummock Water Aureole 70
cyclothem 9, 109, 130–4

dacite 6, 55–9
Dalegarth 46–51
Dalton Beds **35**, 40
Davidsonina carbonaria 17
Delepinia carinata 40
Dent Subgroup 6–8, 23, 27–33, **125**

Derwent Water 76–82, 95–100
Devensian **2**, 11, 63, 72, 89–94, 95–6
Devoke Water 46–53
Devonian **x**, 1–3, 7–9, 89–91, 102, **125**, 127
Dibunophyllum 17–18, 37, 134
Diphyphylloid 133
Diphyphyllum 134
dolerite 82, 96, 99, 120, 123, 129
dolomite 1, 35, 66, 82, 128
drumlin 11, 43, 77, 96–100
Dufton 123–5
Dufton Pike 124–7
Dufton Shales 125–6
dune deposit 115–22
dyke 7–8, 83–7, 120

Eagle Crag Tuffs 55–8
Ennerdale 54–7
Ennerdale Granophyre **2**, 7, **70**, 71
epidote 22–3, 61
erratics 13, 63, 84, 126
escarpment 12–18, 37–8, 119–29
Eskdale 7, 46–53, 61
Eskdale Granite **2**, 7–8, 46–53
esker 99
evaporate **2**, 10, 63
Eycott Group **x**, **2**, 5, 7

Faulds Brow Quarry 110–13
feldspar 20–5, 44, 47–53, 57, 84, 104, 126–7
Fleetwith Pike 70–4
flow-banding 23, 57, 61
fluorite 22, 53, 76
flute mark 23, 32, 44, 72
Friar's Crag 96–9

galena 76, 105, 128
ganister 132–3
garnet 22, 84, 86
Gatesgarth 69–70, 73–4
Gaythorn cyclothem 131–4
George Gill 121–2
Gigantella 114
Gigantoproductus 18, 132
glacifluvial 98, 123, 125
Glenderaterra Beck 101–5
Grange in Borrowdale 75–6, 82
granite **2**, 7–8, 13–15, 19–25, 46–53, 74,
101–6, 125–7
granodiorite 46–7, 52, 68, 102
graptolite 4, 41, 43, 126
Great Rundale 123–5, 127–8
greisen 47–53, 102
greywacke 4, 14, 25, 27, 32–3, 44, 68, 101,
104
gypsum 10, 63, 65

hanging valley 72, 100
Hartsop 89–94
Haycock 54–8
hematite 20, 36, 38–40, 46–53, 117

Hercynian 9
High Cup Nick 129
Hoff 121
Holkerian Stage 16–18
Honister **70**, 71–4
Hope Beck Slates 69
hornfels 24, 49, 58, 102–4

ignimbrite 6, 54–61, 127
imbricate 15, 121
inlier 1, 123–4

Jaws of Borrowdale 76–7

kame 99
kaolinite 22, 104
Keswick 75–6, 95–100, 107
kettle hole 76, 81
Kirkstile Slates 69
Kirkstone Pass 88–94
Knipe Scar Limestone 18, **131**–2
Knock Pike 124–5, 129
Koninckophyllum 40

La'al Ratty 51
lateral moraine, *see* moraine
limestone pavement 18
limestone **2**–3, 7, 9, 12–18, 25, 31, 33, 43–
40, 66, 107–14, 121, **125**–9, 130–4
Linoprotonia 7
Lithostrotion 17, 37, 38, 113–14
Loch Lomond Stadial 11, 90–4, 95–6
Lonsdaleia 114, 134
Loweswater Flags 69, 72

Magnesian Limestone 66
malachite 105
Marchon factory 62–5
Maulds Meaburn cyclothem **131**
Mell Fell Conglomerate 8
Mellbreak 71
Melmerby Scar Limestone 125, 127
meltwater channels 62, 82, 125, 132
metamorphic aureole 7, 102
metamorphism, regional 102–4; thermal
(contact) 4, 22, 84, 101–4
metasomatism 20, 22, 102
mica 47–53, 102
microgranite **2**, 7, 44–5, 46–53, 71, 125–6
molybdenite 22, 53
moraine 11, 76–82, 90–4
mudstone **2**, 4, 7, 13–15, 23, 27–33, 43–5,
53, 69, 101–4, 126, 128
Murton 123–4
Murton Formation **125**, 127
muscovite 102, 126

Nab Gill Mine 45–51
Namurian **x**, **2**, 9, 109
Nemistium 114
New Red Sandstone 62–8

Index

Ordovician **x**, 1–8, 25, 26–33, 56, 84, 102
orogeny 4, 8–10, 42, 70, 84, 102
orthoclase 14, 20–5
Orton 12–18, 130–1
Orton Group **125**, 127
Orton Scar 13–18, 131–2
Outer Pennine Fault **x**, 125–6
outlier 49

Palaeosmilia 18, 40, 134
Park Limestone 36–40
Pennine Escarpment 1, 123–9
Pennine Way 123, 126–9
Penrith Sandstone **2**, 10, 115–22
periglacial 90–4, 95, 99
Permo-Triassic **x**, 1, **2–3**, 9–10, 62–8, 115–22, 123–6
phenocryst 20, 44, 47–9, 52, 57, 84, 126
plagioclase 20, 47, 102
Plumpton 34, 38–40
porphyritic 20–3, 47, 57, 71, 84, 126
porphyroblast 102
porphyry 126
Potts Beck Limestone 16–18
pryite 22–3, 27, 76, 110–11
pyroclastic fall, *see* tuff
pyroclastic surge, *see* tuff
pyromorphite 105
pyroxene 31, 57

quartz 14, 22–3, 29, 47–53, 67–8, 76, 84, 86, 104–5, 117, 119, 126, 127
Quaternary 10–11, 88–94

Ravenstonedale Trough 13
recessional moraine, *see* moraine
Red Hill Oolite 35, 39–40
Red Pike Andesite **55**
Red Pike (Wasdale) 54–61
Rhizocorallum 66
rhyodacite 61
rhyolite 6, 23, 25, 127
River Eden 119
roche moutonnée 30, 43, 49, 72, 76–82, 84
Rosthwaite in Borrowdale 75–82

sandstone **2–3**, 4, 7–11, 13–18, 25, 31–3, 43–5, 56, 63–8, 69, 72–3, 107–11, 113, 125–9, 130–4
Schizodus 66
Scoat Tarn **55**
Seatallan Dacite 56–9
sericite 47
shale **2**, 7, 9, 13–18, 25, 35, 38, 65, 107, 109–11, 113, 125–6, 130–4
Shap Granite **2**, 7, 13–18, 19–25, 125–7
sill **2**, 5, 7, 44, 56–7, 123–5, 128–9
siltstone **2**, 4, 23, 25, 27, 43–5, 56, 126–7
Silurian **x**, **2–3**, 6–8, 13–14, 19–25, 26–33, 37–8, 72, 102
Sinen Gill 101–5

Siphodendron 133–4
Skiddaw Granite **2**, 74, 101–6
Skiddaw Group **x**, 1–6, 8, 46–53, 69–74, 75, 96, 99–100, 101–4, 125
slate 4, 8, 14, 69, 74, 82, 99, 102, 104
slickenside 33, 36, 86
sole mark 28, 32, 72
specularite, *see* hematite
sphalerite 76
Spirifer 133
St Bees 62–8
St Bees Shale **2**, 65
St Bees Sandstone 63–8, 125
Stonethwaite in Borrowdale 77–81
submerged forest 68
Syringopora 17, 113

Tarn Hows 26–33
terminal moraine, *see* moraine
Tertiary **3**, 10, 89
Thirlmere 83–7
Threlkeld 7, 101
till 11, 52, 63, 91–2, 96–9
topaz 47, 49, 53
Torver 41–3
tourmaline 47, 72
trace fossil 66, 111
trap scenery 58–9
trilobite 111, 126
trough end 71, 74
truncated spur 71
tufa 133
tuff **2**, 5, 49, 52–3, 54–61, 66, 71–4, 83, 86–7, 127; air fall 5, 54–6; pyroclastic fall 6, 58; pyroclastic surge 6, 60, 127
turbidite 7, 32–3, 41, 69–70, 129
Tynebottom Limestone **125**, 128–9

Uldale 107–14
Ullswater 1, 9, 89
Ulverston 34–40
unconformity 13, 19, 22, 27, 62, 65–6, 74, 120
Upper Carboniferous 62, 65–7
Urswick Limestone 36–40

Vale of Eden 9, 115–22, 127–30

Warnscale Bottom 71, 73, 74
Wasdale 5, 54–61
Watendlath 82, 100
Westphalian **x**, 2, 9, 62–4
Whin Sill **2**, 123–5, 128–9
Whitehaven **x**, 9, 62
Windermere Group **2–3**, 6–8, 14, 20–6, 26–33, 41–5
Wray Castle Formation 28–33, 43–5

Zaphrentis 113
Zoophycos 110, 111